LeadingEdge *Teams*

Ahead of the **Curve**

How to be a thriving 'A+' Leader in the fast paced,
ever-changing landscape of business today

30-Day Self-Leadership Journal

ANNIE HYMAN PRATT

LUMINARE PRESS

WWW.LUMINAREPRESS.COM

Ahead of the Curve
*How to be a thriving 'A' Player in the fast-paced,
ever-changing landscape of business today*
Leading Edge Teams Self-Leadership Journal #1
www.leadingedgeteams.com
Copyright © 2020 | Annie Hyman Pratt,
Leading Edge Teams

Printed in the United States of America

Cover Design: Nina Leis and Jim McGonigal
Luminare Press
442 Charnelton St.
Eugene, OR 97401
www.luminarepress.com

LCCN: 2019918877
ISBN: 978-1-64388-190-4

To my team, thank you for suggesting that we create this journal, doing the heavy lifting to make it happen, and for expertly influencing me to do my part even though we have more than full plates!

Having this journal enables us to more positively and easily impact today's business leaders, and it would not have come to be without your amazing contributions.

TABLE OF CONTENTS

Gratitude

Thank you to all who contributed to the creation of this journal.

I especially want to thank the entrepreneurs who first requested that I develop a leadership program. Working with you and your leaders through the ups and downs of the entrepreneurial journey, has been both a challenge and a great joy. The 'A+' Leader Development Program and Mastermind is what started me in specializing in the "people part" of business and is something I am so very proud of. It truly wouldn't have come to be without you and your support and belief in me.

Thank you to my husband David. You are an inspiring entrepreneur and the best partner I could have ever hoped for. Your support and patience has been such a gift.

To my parents Herb and Mona Hyman, thank you for your incredible example of courage in the business world and everywhere else. And to my children, thank you for being a big part of the "why" in everything I do.

"Only from oneself has one the right to ask everything.
What we receive from others remains a gift."

—*ALBERT SCHWEITZER*

Introduction

Thank you for purchasing this journal. Our commitment is to provide you with the tools and skills you need to be an 'A' Player, and even more importantly, an 'A+' Leader, in today's rapidly changing business landscape. This is more important than ever because the old model of top down authority and control does not work anymore. It's an antiquated approach that cripples team performance and business growth, because team members can't wait for instruction and hold off decision-making, while the few people at the top do the vast majority of the thinking. The old "follow the rules and do what I say" is a terrible way to get people to think on their own and take the most effective action.

This authority and control way must be replaced with an inclusive team approach, one in which individuals can bring their best thinking and performance forward. This creates a culture where team members and leadership work together effectively to drive the business growth and achieve the company vision and goals.

Critical thinking and effective action is needed at every level of the organization for a business to achieve growth and sustain success today. It is no longer enough to have team members who just do the functional tasks they're assigned, because needs and circumstances change too fast. Everyone needs the ability to constantly adjust what they're doing.

Also, business needs all team members to take responsibility for achieving the results that their tasks are designed to support—doing tasks without minding the actual outcomes always breaks down. And the consequences of poor work at the task level causes the entire organization to go into crisis mode—doing the exact things that they hired their teams to do instead of the higher level work that the business desperately needs.

The solution is to REPLACE the Authority and Control Paradigm, with the ACE Team Triangle (Alignment, Collective Agreement and Effective Action), enabling team members to think critically, make good decisions, take strong action, and ultimately to achieve the fastest and best results.

Whether you are an entrepreneur or key leader in a company, the demands of business today require you to make this shift. Because without a strategic team, your business has an extremely low probability of surviving, let alone thriving.

Making this shift starts with YOU! And that is great news because controlling others doesn't work anyhow! You can play a big part, if not the biggest part, in creating positive company change because your leadership development is entirely in your domain.

So this is where we start, teaching YOU the essential skill of Self-Leadership.

This journal covers the essential skills and key mindset shifts needed to master Self-Leadership. This journal is also meant to help you create a Self-Leadership practice, because the more consistently you practice these skills, the more quickly they'll become a reliable, automatic, habit for you, freeing your thinking to focus on creativity and innovation.

As you practice these leadership skills, we think you will be surprised at how quickly you'll see the positive impact you are creating.

Welcome to Leadership!

P.S. For the skeptics who think that they can wait to shift until their team is "just a little more competent or well trained," or who think they need to hire "better people"—we encourage you to embrace Self-Leadership as a life raft in your current sea of doing too many things yourself. Without Self-Leadership, you will eventually drown, no matter how good of a swimmer you are.

You need a highly effective team, and your foundation is Self-Leadership. Because the best 'A+' Players want to work for 'A+' Leaders, which is what Self-Leadership is all about.

How To Get The Most From This Journal

First, congratulations for making the commitment to explore and improve your Self-Leadership skills over the next 30 days, and beyond. All of us at Leading Edge Teams hope that this journal may serve as a catalyst of change and encouragement for your 'A+' Leader development.

There are three sections to this journal in which you will do daily practice exercises. To achieve the fastest and most sustainable results from these exercises, we encourage you to do these as instructed for 30 consecutive days in the order they are laid out. The repetition of daily practice will be the best support you can give yourself while changing your habits. If the language of any of the questions fails to resonate with your experience, feel free to substitute phrases that you can better relate to. The key is to keep moving forward through your daily practice. Building new habits takes dedication to change. Your effort and time will be well rewarded!

Get Started: Take our "Online Self-Leadership Quiz" to uncover your own "Team Leadership Superpower" before you start Section One. A link to access the quiz is provided at the end of the next section.

We hope you enjoy taking this leadership journey with us and we would enjoy hearing from you. If you would like to say "Hi," share your experience or find more team leadership tools, join us on Facebook www.facebook.com/anniehymanpratt/.

—Annie and the Leading Edge Team

My Self-Assessment

A successful growth journey starts with a solid assessment of where you are starting from. Only then can you really recognize how far you've come at the end of the journey.

First, please answer the questions below to set your intentions and to ground yourself for the next 30 days...

Next, please take the "Online Leadership Assessment Quiz" to get a comprehensive picture of your leadership strengths and growth opportunities...

So, take a few moments and answer the questions here, and then hop online and take the quiz.

Let the journey begin!

Leadership Intention Questions:

▶ Why are you interested in growing your leadership (with self and others)?

_____

_____

‣ Are there any specific challenges or growth areas in your leadership that you want to address?

‣ What do you hope to achieve in the next 30 days through this process?

▶ What would you be doing differently if you achieve those goals? What would it look like?

_____

_____

_____

_____

_____

_____

▶ What three leadership strengths have you particularly admired in others that you would like to cultivate more of for yourself?

_____

_____

_____

_____

_____

_____

Take the Online Leadership Assessment Quiz:

https://leadingedgeteams.com/leadership-assessment-quiz

Additional Thoughts

My Self-Awareness

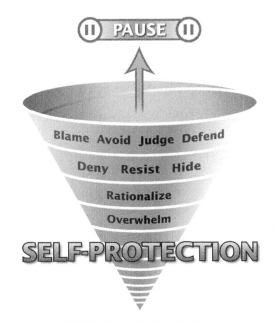

"Perhaps the most important single cause of a person's success or failure has to do with the question of what he believes about himself."

—*ARTHUR W. COMBS*

Lesson 1

Humans are easily the most difficult part of building and operating a successful business. They're extraordinary when performing well, but getting them to perform well is more difficult and complex than most people understand, especially when operating in a team environment (meaning, not solo).

Leaders are generally great action takers, taking lots of steps to improve their business. But when they have a team, those efforts often get unintentionally derailed by team members who don't understand what the leader is going for, or are impacted in a negative way for their own role.

A classic example is when leaders implement systems and processes only to have their team completely ignore them and continue doing their own, ineffective thing. Or when leaders believe they've clearly delegated a task, but the team member does something different, and gets a disappointing result. Or when challenges hit, and your team sits back and waits for you to make all the decisions while things deteriorate from inaction.

In all these examples, it seems like the problem is clearly with the OTHER team members not doing the right thing, but human cooperation and performance is complex. How you interact with your team is much more important than you probably assume.

You might have the urge to debate us on that point, sharing how your team really is incompetent even when your leadership is quite strong, but we encourage you to think completely differently about this.

We've found that leadership capability (your behaviors and communications) has an incredibly direct and rapid impact on how your team behaves and performs. Because of that, you can leverage tremendous positive growth and change by addressing and shifting behavior—YOUR BEHAVIOR.

But first we need to understand a bit about human behavior and how it really works. Put very simply, humans have three types of behavior:

1. Intentional behavior that has conscious thinking behind it
2. Reactive behavior that is generated automatically by the amygdala (the emotional center of the brain) and is most often meant to protect you and ensure your survival
3. Habitual behavior that is also generated automatically, so that you don't waste your conscious thinking on repetitive activities

As humans, we spend much of our day in automatic behavior mode, which is needed because our conscious thinking paired with deliberate actions take a lot of effort and energy. But these automatic behaviors, especially the ones that are emotionally reactive, can be especially problematic when humans are working together to achieve results.

The human amygdala is often described as a "threat detecting machine." Whenever it senses a threat in the environment, regardless if it's a grizzly bear headed your way or a team member accidentally causing a financial loss, it will spring into action by spinning up your emotions and adrenaline, causing you to take the most immediate action possible to deal with the threat.

This works great when the threat is a grizzly bear (run away as fast as possible), but it works terribly for today's business threats which are much more complex and need logical thinking and cooperation to solve. Unfortunately, the amygdala doesn't know the difference, and it will stir up your emotions for the business threat too, causing you to react without thinking and go into fight, flight, freeze, or please mode, with the people you most need to help resolve the threat or repair the problem!

Fight, flight, freeze, and please behaviors are meant to protect us FROM threats, including if the threat is other people. But in business, we need to engage the opposite behaviors during threats, stress, and challenge. We need people to cooperate and work together while engaging their best thinking. None of that can happen when humans are emotionally reactive.

So, to level up your own leadership skills, you must begin by taking a look at your reactive behaviors in the face of stress, challenge, and change. You need to know your default self-protective behaviors. These are the ones you don't have to think about as your primitive brain jumps into action.

In the CcORE Empowerment Process, which is our core teaching tool, the lower Self-Protection triangle demonstrates the downward spiral of emotionally reactive behaviors. Nothing good happens when we automatically fall into these protective behaviors—and yet we're compelled to go to those behaviors because according to the primitive brain, we are doing what we must do to get safe. But these reactive behaviors destroy our ability to show up in the thinking, productive, and creative way that allows us to get the bigger outcomes we want for ourselves, our lives, and our business.

When you become aware of your own reactive behaviors, you have a key business advantage because you can choose to do something conscious instead of being blind to your default behaviors. Strong self-awareness enables you to shift out of reaction mode and choose a productive leadership action instead. As a result of doing this work—you will navigate the everyday challenges of business with greater ease. You will be able to think clearly and choose the best action for the situation you are facing in the moment.

In this first lesson, our main objective is for you to develop the ability to PAUSE before your emotional reaction takes you off course. The power of this PAUSE is that it creates a space for you to regulate your emotions so you can then choose your behavior.

Every human engages in reactive behaviors. Not only is it NOT wrong to find yourself there, but it's your hard-wired, expected response to stress and challenge. However, unchecked emotional Self-Protection causes us to separate from rather than connect to others, which is vital to teamwork and success.

As represented in our model, Self-Protective behavior has a tendency to spiral down. It leads to conflicts, poor decisions, disruption of workflow, and repeating crisis. Each of these take time to repair and recover from, thereby impacting your forward trajectory. Constructive, good thinking is not available when you are operating from spiraling emotions.

Here are some common tell-tale signs that you are in Reactive Thinking and Self-Protection:

- Holding the perspective of right or wrong (you're right, they're wrong)
- Blaming or judging others or yourself
- Defending yourself or others
- Intensely holding your position, resisting any exploration of other positions
- Avoiding or denying an issue, or your part in it
- Seeing yourself as a victim who has no ability whatsoever to influence the situation

It's important to know these signs and to also look for the less obvious, more stealth ways that you may be in Self-Protection mode. Because this mode harms your performance, no matter how low-level it is.

Annie Hyman Pratt

Let's look at an example of Self-Protective behaviors in business. Imagine you are in an important team meeting and a teammate questions the progress of a big project you are leading. They express concern that it should be further along, implying your performance is lacking. Let's add one more stressful element: your CEO is in the meeting and hearing this without any other context.

How would you feel in that moment and what would you do? A Self-Protective reaction would be to defend yourself and go into explaining every aspect of what you are doing and why. This leads to a debate with the other team member, where you both engage in blaming, rationalizing, and defending, and the meeting spirals off course. Now neither of you look good and your CEO is losing confidence and questioning the team's ability to resolve issues productively, which is a major factor in performance.

Until you are truly aware of how and when you fall into a reactive state, you will not be able to shift or change your behavior to get the results you want. You might be thinking that this really isn't true for you; however, think of a time when someone you care about was saying things and making decisions in an emotional state. How good was their thinking and decision-making? Probably not good at all, and it's the same for you. This is why it's imperative that you recognize your hard-wired, protective behaviors.

Building the muscle of self-awareness and your ability to PAUSE before you react, sets you up to make a different choice. It levels up your leadership, allowing you to shift out of reactivity to engage in critical thinking and effective interaction instead.

The goal of this lesson is to raise your self-awareness and build your PAUSE muscle when you get "triggered" (i.e. stressed, challenged, angry, fearful, etc.) instead of going into immediate reaction.

For the next few days, you will practice **Self-Awareness–Pause–Choice**. When you experience a trigger, you'll take a moment, and self-regulate your emotions. Self-regulation is key, as it de-escalates the emotional energy that would otherwise drive your actions. Don't skip this step. There are many ways to self-regulate; here are just a few.

Some common ways to self-regulate:

- Take a break
- Walk around the block
- Take a few deep breaths and a timeout
- Take your dog for a walk
- Count to ten
- Take an exercise break
- Dance it out

While you are learning to become more aware of your emotional reactivity, take the time to notice what your behavior looks like when you are in Self-Protection. Each of us have favorite "Self-Protection hang-outs" when we are stressed and challenged—our strongest default habits.

Some of the behaviors demonstrated in Self-Protection are to avoid, hide, ignore, blame, judge, criticize, rationalize, and justify. When in Self-Protection you may feel powerless. It can feel like circumstances are happening to you. In business, this looks like being in a mode of constantly putting out fires and moving from crisis to crisis. Operating in this way leads to a sense of overwhelm which may then spiral to mental and emotional burnout.

Being familiar with how you operate from Self-Protection gives you the ability to shift out of it faster.

Overwhelm and burnout is becoming an epidemic in our current business climate. Practicing **Self-Awareness–Pause–Choice** is the key to a different way of being in business—one that is healthy and sustainable for you and your employees.

This first ten days is the start of a powerful foundation of change. Give it your best.

"When we are interacting with people, we have to take responsibility for our own Self-Leadership. The more we demonstrate it, the more people are free to do the same."

—*ANNIE HYMAN PRATT*

▶▶▶

Day 1

▶ Were there any times or situations today where you noticed yourself being reactive or engaging in Self-Protective behaviors?

_____

_____

_____

_____

_____

▶ What was the situation(s)? Why did it matter?

_____

_____

_____

_____

_____

▶ What did you do to regulate your emotions? (i.e. take a break, take a walk, breathe...)

_____

_____

_____

_____

_____

▶ What were you feeling? Can you describe those feelings fully?

_____

_____

_____

_____

_____

▶ How did you react or behave? What did you do in the situation?

_____

_____

_____

_____

_____

▶ Were you able to notice yourself in Self-Protection? Did you stop, pause and/or take a break instead of escalating or increasing your engagement in reactive behaviors? If so, how did that go?

▶ What outcome were you intending to achieve in this situation? What were you going for? How did the situation turn out?

▶ Is there anything you would do differently next time?

▶ Is there a pattern in your Self-Protection that you notice? What are the behaviors you tend to go to most? (Remember, everybody has habitual reactive behaviors, it's not bad, just something you want to become aware of so that you have a chance to shift.)

_____

_____

_____

_____

_____

_____

▶ Examples of self-protective behaviors:

Avoid	**Deny**
Resist	**Judge**
Ignore	**Rationalize**
Blame	**Hide**
Story	**Overwhelm**
Defend	**Manipulation**

Additional Thoughts

"Choice is the power point. You always have a choice. Thinking you don't is an illusion."

—ANNIE HYMAN PRATT

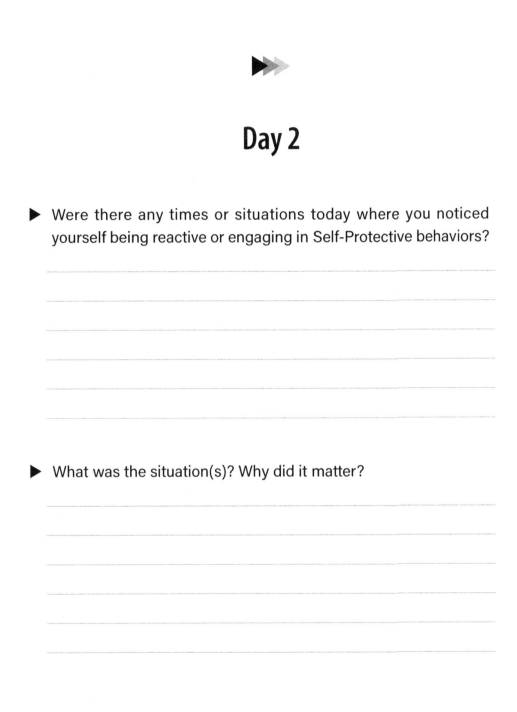

Day 2

▶ Were there any times or situations today where you noticed yourself being reactive or engaging in Self-Protective behaviors?

_____

_____

_____

_____

_____

_____

▶ What was the situation(s)? Why did it matter?

_____

_____

_____

_____

_____

_____

▶ What did you do to regulate your emotions? (i.e. take a break, take a walk, breathe...)

_____

_____

_____

_____

_____

▶ What were you feeling? Can you describe those feelings fully?

_____

_____

_____

_____

_____

▶ How did you react or behave? What did you do in the situation?

_____

_____

_____

_____

_____

Annie Hyman Pratt

▶ Were you able to notice yourself in Self-Protection? Did you stop, pause and/or take a break instead of escalating or increasing your engagement in reactive behaviors? If so, how did that go?

_____

_____

_____

_____

_____

▶ What outcome were you intending to achieve in this situation? What were you going for? How did the situation turn out?

_____

_____

_____

_____

_____

▶ Is there anything you would do differently next time?

_____

_____

_____

_____

▶ Is there a pattern in your Self-Protection that you notice? What are the behaviors you tend to go to most? (Remember, everybody has habitual reactive behaviors, it's not bad, just something you want to become aware of so that you have a chance to shift.)

_____

_____

_____

_____

_____

_____

▶ Examples of self-protective behaviors:

Avoid	**Deny**
Resist	**Judge**
Ignore	**Rationalize**
Blame	**Hide**
Story	**Overwhelm**
Defend	**Manipulation**

Additional Thoughts

"If you can't get really good at getting out of the Self-Protection Triangle and up to Self-Leadership, then you become a severe limitation to growing your company and your team. At some point, it becomes show-stopping."

—*ANNIE HYMAN PRATT*

Day 3

▶ Were there any times or situations today where you noticed yourself being reactive or engaging in Self-Protective behaviors?

_____

_____

_____

_____

_____

▶ What was the situation(s)? Why did it matter?

_____

_____

_____

_____

▶ What did you do to regulate your emotions? (i.e. take a break, take a walk, breathe...)

_____

_____

_____

_____

_____

_____

▶ What were you feeling? Can you describe those feelings fully?

_____

_____

_____

_____

_____

_____

▶ How did you react or behave? What did you do in the situation?

_____

_____

_____

_____

_____

_____

▶ Were you able to notice yourself in Self-Protection? Did you stop, pause and/or take a break instead of escalating or increasing your engagement in reactive behaviors? If so, how did that go?

_____

_____

_____

_____

_____

_____

▶ What outcome were you intending to achieve in this situation? What were you going for? How did the situation turn out?

_____

_____

_____

_____

_____

_____

▶ Is there anything you would do differently next time?

_____

_____

_____

_____

_____

▶ Is there a pattern in your Self-Protection that you notice? What are the behaviors you tend to go to most? (Remember, everybody has habitual reactive behaviors, it's not bad, just something you want to become aware of so that you have a chance to shift.)

_____

_____

_____

_____

_____

_____

▶ Examples of self-protective behaviors:

Avoid	**Deny**
Resist	**Judge**
Ignore	**Rationalize**
Blame	**Hide**
Story	**Overwhelm**
Defend	**Manipulation**

Additional Thoughts

"Only you can solve your overwhelm."

—*ANNIE HYMAN PRATT*

Day 4

▶ Were there any times or situations today where you noticed yourself being reactive or engaging in Self-Protective behaviors?

_____

_____

_____

_____

_____

▶ What was the situation(s)? Why did it matter?

_____

_____

_____

_____

_____

▶ What did you do to regulate your emotions? (i.e. take a break, take a walk, breathe...)

_____

_____

_____

_____

_____

▶ What were you feeling? Can you describe those feelings fully?

_____

_____

_____

_____

_____

▶ How did you react or behave? What did you do in the situation?

_____

_____

_____

_____

_____

Annie Hyman Pratt

▶ Were you able to notice yourself in Self-Protection? Did you stop, pause and/or take a break instead of escalating or increasing your engagement in reactive behaviors? If so, how did that go?

▶ What outcome were you intending to achieve in this situation? What were you going for? How did the situation turn out?

▶ Is there anything you would do differently next time?

▶ Is there a pattern in your Self-Protection that you notice? What are the behaviors you tend to go to most? (Remember, everybody has habitual reactive behaviors, it's not bad, just something you want to become aware of so that you have a chance to shift.)

_____

_____

_____

_____

_____

_____

▶ Examples of self-protective behaviors:

Avoid	**Deny**
Resist	**Judge**
Ignore	**Rationalize**
Blame	**Hide**
Story	**Overwhelm**
Defend	**Manipulation**

Additional Thoughts

"What works for you to get back to Self-Leadership?
Athletes have rituals that get them back into a good
mindset. They can move on from the last bad play. Athletes
make mistakes all the time and they've learned how to get
themselves good with it so they can focus on the rest of the
game, not what's just happened."

—ANNIE HYMAN PRATT

Day 5

▶ Were there any times or situations today where you noticed yourself being reactive or engaging in Self-Protective behaviors?

_____

_____

_____

_____

_____

▶ What was the situation(s)? Why did it matter?

_____

_____

_____

_____

_____

▶ What did you do to regulate your emotions? (i.e. take a break, take a walk, breathe...)

_____

_____

_____

_____

_____

▶ What were you feeling? Can you describe those feelings fully?

_____

_____

_____

_____

_____

▶ How did you react or behave? What did you do in the situation?

_____

_____

_____

_____

_____

▶ Were you able to notice yourself in Self-Protection? Did you stop, pause and/or take a break instead of escalating or increasing your engagement in reactive behaviors? If so, how did that go?

_____

_____

_____

_____

_____

▶ What outcome were you intending to achieve in this situation? What were you going for? How did the situation turn out?

_____

_____

_____

_____

_____

▶ Is there anything you would do differently next time?

_____

_____

_____

_____

_____

► Is there a pattern in your Self-Protection that you notice? What are the behaviors you tend to go to most? (Remember, everybody has habitual reactive behaviors, it's not bad, just something you want to become aware of so that you have a chance to shift.)

_____

_____

_____

_____

_____

► Examples of self-protective behaviors:

Avoid	**Deny**
Resist	**Judge**
Ignore	**Rationalize**
Blame	**Hide**
Story	**Overwhelm**
Defend	**Manipulation**

Additional Thoughts

"What makes for personal accountability is when you're safe enough and willing to risk taking intentional action versus reaction and self-protective behaviors."

—*ANNIE HYMAN PRATT*

Day 6

▶ Were there any times or situations today where you noticed yourself being reactive or engaging in Self-Protective behaviors?

_____

_____

_____

_____

_____

_____

▶ What was the situation(s)? Why did it matter?

_____

_____

_____

_____

_____

▶ What did you do to regulate your emotions? (i.e. take a break, take a walk, breathe...)

_____

_____

_____

_____

_____

▶ What were you feeling? Can you describe those feelings fully?

_____

_____

_____

_____

_____

▶ How did you react or behave? What did you do in the situation?

_____

_____

_____

_____

_____

▶ Were you able to notice yourself in Self-Protection? Did you stop, pause and/or take a break instead of escalating or increasing your engagement in reactive behaviors? If so, how did that go?

▶ What outcome were you intending to achieve in this situation? What were you going for? How did the situation turn out?

▶ Is there anything you would do differently next time?

► Is there a pattern in your Self-Protection that you notice? What are the behaviors you tend to go to most? (Remember, everybody has habitual reactive behaviors, it's not bad, just something you want to become aware of so that you have a chance to shift.)

_____

_____

_____

_____

_____

_____

► Examples of self-protective behaviors:

Avoid	**Deny**
Resist	**Judge**
Ignore	**Rationalize**
Blame	**Hide**
Story	**Overwhelm**
Defend	**Manipulation**

"Think of behaviors, especially the collective ones, as your culture. When people say, 'culture eats strategy for breakfast,' they're talking about the behavior piece."

—*ANNIE HYMAN PRATT*

▶▶▶

Day 7

▶ Were there any times or situations today where you noticed yourself being reactive or engaging in Self-Protective behaviors?

_____

_____

_____

_____

_____

_____

▶ What was the situation(s)? Why did it matter?

_____

_____

_____

_____

_____

▶ What did you do to regulate your emotions? (i.e. take a break, take a walk, breathe...)

_____

_____

_____

_____

_____

_____

▶ What were you feeling? Can you describe those feelings fully?

_____

_____

_____

_____

_____

_____

▶ How did you react or behave? What did you do in the situation?

_____

_____

_____

_____

_____

_____

▶ Were you able to notice yourself in Self-Protection? Did you stop, pause and/or take a break instead of escalating or increasing your engagement in reactive behaviors? If so, how did that go?

_____

_____

_____

_____

_____

▶ What outcome were you intending to achieve in this situation? What were you going for? How did the situation turn out?

_____

_____

_____

_____

_____

_____

▶ Is there anything you would do differently next time?

_____

_____

_____

_____

▶ Is there a pattern in your Self-Protection that you notice? What are the behaviors you tend to go to most? (Remember, everybody has habitual reactive behaviors, it's not bad, just something you want to become aware of so that you have a chance to shift.)

_____

_____

_____

_____

_____

_____

▶ Examples of self-protective behaviors:

Avoid	**Deny**
Resist	**Judge**
Ignore	**Rationalize**
Blame	**Hide**
Story	**Overwhelm**
Defend	**Manipulation**

Annie Hyman Pratt

Additional Thoughts

"It takes some time to be able to articulate the behaviors
you want. But, when you know the behaviors you
don't want, then you just need to think about
what it is you *do* want."

—*ANNIE HYMAN PRATT*

▶▶▶

Day 8

▶ Were there any times or situations today where you noticed yourself being reactive or engaging in Self-Protective behaviors?

_____

_____

_____

_____

_____

▶ What was the situation(s)? Why did it matter?

_____

_____

_____

_____

_____

_____

▶ What did you do to regulate your emotions? (i.e. take a break, take a walk, breathe...)

_____

_____

_____

_____

_____

▶ What were you feeling? Can you describe those feelings fully?

_____

_____

_____

_____

_____

▶ How did you react or behave? What did you do in the situation?

_____

_____

_____

_____

_____

▶ Were you able to notice yourself in Self-Protection? Did you stop, pause and/or take a break instead of escalating or increasing your engagement in reactive behaviors? If so, how did that go?

_____

_____

_____

_____

_____

_____

▶ What outcome were you intending to achieve in this situation? What were you going for? How did the situation turn out?

_____

_____

_____

_____

_____

_____

▶ Is there anything you would do differently next time?

_____

_____

_____

_____

_____

▶ Is there a pattern in your Self-Protection that you notice? What are the behaviors you tend to go to most? (Remember, everybody has habitual reactive behaviors, it's not bad, just something you want to become aware of so that you have a chance to shift.)

_____

_____

_____

_____

_____

_____

▶ Examples of self-protective behaviors:

Avoid	**Deny**
Resist	**Judge**
Ignore	**Rationalize**
Blame	**Hide**
Story	**Overwhelm**
Defend	**Manipulation**

Additional Thoughts

"Learning all of this is like learning how to play a sport. At first, it's a mess. But as you get better, you start to feel more confident about playing the game; you've created a lot of good technical habits, and you evolve as your game evolves. It's all about building confidence to know you can play the game no matter how technical it gets."

—ANNIE HYMAN PRATT

Day 9

▶ Were there any times or situations today where you noticed yourself being reactive or engaging in Self-Protective behaviors?

_____

_____

_____

_____

_____

▶ What was the situation(s)? Why did it matter?

_____

_____

_____

_____

_____

▶ What did you do to regulate your emotions? (i.e. take a break, take a walk, breathe...)

_____

_____

_____

_____

_____

▶ What were you feeling? Can you describe those feelings fully?

_____

_____

_____

_____

_____

▶ How did you react or behave? What did you do in the situation?

_____

_____

_____

_____

_____

▶ Were you able to notice yourself in Self-Protection? Did you stop, pause and/or take a break instead of escalating or increasing your engagement in reactive behaviors? If so, how did that go?

▶ What outcome were you intending to achieve in this situation? What were you going for? How did the situation turn out?

▶ Is there anything you would do differently next time?

n your Self-Protection that you notice? What are
u tend to go to most? (Remember, everybody has
ive behaviors, it's not bad, just something you want
aware of so that you have a chance to shift.)

_____

_____

_____

_____

_____

_____

▶ Examples of self-protective behaviors:

Avoid	**Deny**
Resist	**Judge**
Ignore	**Rationalize**
Blame	**Hide**
Story	**Overwhelm**
Defend	**Manipulation**

Additional Thoughts

"Never underestimate the phrase 'you can do this.'
It's incredibly powerful."

—*ANNIE HYMAN PRATT*

▶▶▶

Day 10

▶ Were there any times or situations today where you noticed yourself being reactive or engaging in Self-Protective behaviors?

_____

_____

_____

_____

_____

▶ What was the situation(s)? Why did it matter?

_____

_____

_____

_____

_____

▶ What did you do to regulate your emotions? (i.e. take a break, take a walk, breathe...)

_____

_____

_____

_____

_____

▶ What were you feeling? Can you describe those feelings fully?

_____

_____

_____

_____

_____

▶ How did you react or behave? What did you do in the situation?

_____

_____

_____

_____

_____

▶ Were you able to notice yourself in Self-Protection? Did you stop, pause and/or take a break instead of escalating or increasing your engagement in reactive behaviors? If so, how did that go?

▶ What outcome were you intending to achieve in this situation? What were you going for? How did the situation turn out?

▶ Is there anything you would do differently next time?

▶ Is there a pattern in your Self-Protection that you notice? What are the behaviors you tend to go to most? (Remember, everybody has habitual reactive behaviors, it's not bad, just something you want to become aware of so that you have a chance to shift.)

_____

_____

_____

_____

_____

_____

▶ Examples of self-protective behaviors:

Avoid	**Deny**
Resist	**Judge**
Ignore	**Rationalize**
Blame	**Hide**
Story	**Overwhelm**
Defend	**Manipulation**

10-Day Check-in

My Self Awareness

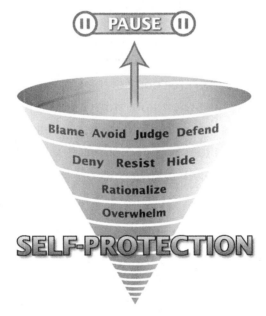

™ © 2020 Annie Hyman Pratt | Leading Edge Teams

So... how did the past ten days go for you?

What would you say is the most important thing that you have learned about yourself and your leadership?

You hopefully recognized some of your limiting reactive behaviors and are experiencing the power of the PAUSE.

Please take a moment now and go to **https://leadingedgeteams.com/ccore-download** and print out a copy of the CcORE Empowerment Process. The leaders in our year-long program find it super handy to post it where they will see it as a daily reminder—especially when stressed and challenged. Keeping this teaching top of mind will help you to build the muscle of Self-Leadership *much faster*.

▶ What I learned about myself in the past ten days...

Additional Thoughts

Working the CcORE Empowerment Process

SELF-LEADERSHIP

E	**Engage**	Engage My Secure Self
R	**Release**	Release Judgement to Compassion
O	**Observe**	Observe My Thoughts & Feelings
C	**Choose**	Choose My Impact
C	**Clarify**	Clarify Situtation

™ © 2020 Annie Hyman Pratt | Leading Edge Teams

"To know others is wisdom; to know yourself
is enlightenment."

—*LAO TZU*

Lesson 2

In the high-pressure atmosphere of business today, it is all too common to feel as if things are moving too fast and out of your control. This is why the leadership skill of managing your emotional reactivity is critical.

In the first section, "My Self-Awareness," you learned about the negative impact of emotional reactivity on your performance and practiced awareness for catching yourself in Self-Protective behaviors. You experienced the power of the PAUSE, which helps regulate your emotions and gives you the space to choose your action.

So now that you've learned to PAUSE... how then can you CHOOSE and act most effectively to set you and your business up for success?

Taking effective action in business almost always requires you to sort and evaluate several pieces of information at once. That usually includes looking at the overall business picture with the others that are involved and impacted (your team), then considering and evaluating options to achieve the desired outcomes. As a leader in these situations your high-level critical thinking is paramount. When you're in anger, resentment, anxiety, or overwhelm your ability to show up well, think, and perform is severely impaired.

With a solid habit of self-regulating your emotions in place, your next step is to anchor your focus on the intended outcomes. This is where you center your focus on the outcome(s) you are going for. Business outcomes serve to align and ground you and your team, no matter what else is happening. When you look at a current situation in relationship to the outcomes you are going for, it pulls things into focus and prepares you to think and act.

Let's now take a look at the CcORE Empowerment Process.

The CcORE Empowerment Process is the critical mindset bridge that prepares you to do your best, most creative, intuitive, effective thinking, and relating. This is an internal process that outlines the steps needed for effective leadership.

In other words, this CcORE Empowerment Process provides a mental and emotional clearing routine before engaging in problem-solving, decision-making, creative thinking, etc. This is especially important before connecting and working with others.

But this process doesn't happen alone. It's important to remember that everything you do in your leadership is grounded in achieving business outcomes. Anchoring in those outcomes is necessary to position yourself to engage the CcORE Empowerment Process.

There are five Steps to the CcORE Empowerment Process:

C	**Clarify Situation**
c	**Choose My Impact**
O	**Observe My Thoughts and Feelings**
R	**Release Judgement to Compassion**
E	**Engage My Secure Self**

When beginning to utilize the CcORE Empowerment Process, we recommend that you start by writing down each step. As you gain proficiency and repetition, you will soon be able to conduct the process mentally without the need to write it all out.

Annie Hyman Pratt

Step 1: Clarify Situation

Make a list of the primary facts of the current situation. Be sure that you list only the clear facts (not your opinions or assumptions about the situation, or the stories and associations you may find yourself attaching through your Self-Protective judgements or fears).

Then look at the list and remind yourself that these are the facts that you cannot change—that you must accept—exactly as is.

Step 2: Choose My Impact

Based on the intended outcomes, clarified facts of the situation, and the current state of the business and team, ask yourself the following:

- How do you want to show up for the best impact?
- How do you most want to contribute to the situation?
- How can you be a positive influence toward achieving the desired outcomes?
- What opinion of yourself do you want to have when you reflect back on your part in this situation?

Step 3: Observe My Thoughts and Feelings

The point of this step is for you to take dominion over your emotions so that they don't control your behavior while still feeling those same emotions. Remember to use the power of the PAUSE for emotional regulation—which is basically bringing down the energy of your emotions to a tolerable level.

You then have the ability to further disempower the negative influence of those emotions on your thinking and actions.

You do this by simply acknowledging those emotions by clearly naming them. Yes, by merely labeling and describing your emotions, you will decrease their power and strengthen your conscious thinking and ability to control your words and actions.

Remember, your emotional feelings are not wrong! They are natural, human, and incredibly important. There is a misperception that you can experience negative emotions AND engage productive thinking and actions. It's not true!

When you are able to emotionally self-regulate and label feelings, you then have ample choice for how you think and act. This is why the step of Observe My Thoughts and Feelings is so important to the CcORE Empowerment Process.

Step 4: Release Judgement to Compassion

Releasing judgement means letting go of all your stories, opinions, evaluations of right/wrong or good/bad, your predictions of the future, and everything else you've attached to the facts of the situation.

It's easiest to recognize judgements by noticing where you've got strong positions of right/wrong or good/bad. Having a strong opinion of being "right," and proving that "rightness" in your mind (or out loud) with evidence from your past negative experiences, is a tell-tale sign of judgement. Automatic projecting of how things will go badly in the future is also judgement. Complaining, criticizing, blaming and defending are strong signs of negative judgements too.

It's helpful to think of releasing judgement in three parts and to ask yourself questions about those parts:

1. Question your CERTAINTY: What do I *really* know?

AKA The "Grand Wizard Test"—*Are you an all-knowing wizard with a crystal ball to predict the future?*

Some questions to ask yourself:

- Do I really understand what's going on here given my single, limited perspective?
- Is it possible that I'm missing facts and perspectives that would impact my thoughts and opinions of this situation?
- Am I making assumptions or attributing meaning that may not actually be true in the situation?
- Do I know and understand all the elements and interconnected factors that lead up to this situation?
- Given how many business factors are out of my control, can I effectively predict the future?
- Is there a way this may positively impact the future of the business, the team, my relationship(s), and myself that I just can't see now?

2. Question your EVALUATION: Is this *definitely* a negative situation?

AKA The "Villain / Victim Test"—*Are you sure this is all bad or wrong with no positive opportunities or consequences, now or in the future? Are you sure this is all about you and that you're all villain or victim?*

Some questions to ask yourself:

- Am I attributing negative intent or selfishness to others' behavior that really isn't there?
- Am I misinterpreting others' behavior as disrespectful of me when they might be in a high level of fear, emotional pain, or self-protection?
- Am I seeing myself as a victim because I can't figure out what to do differently to change or influence my situation?
- Is there a greater opportunity for myself, my team, and the business, hidden in the current challenge—making it highly positive that this came forward?
- Is this situation coming forward because I'm ready to learn and grow and I can't do that while comfy?

- If experiencing conflict or disagreement, is there a way we're actually in agreement beneath the surface issue that I'm not seeing?

3. Question your EFFECTIVENESS: Will my behavior achieve positive results?

AKA The "How's this Working for me? Test"—*Given the facts, am I choosing the thinking, attitudes and behaviors that are most likely to generate a positive result?*

Some questions to ask yourself:

- How am I treating myself and others in this situation—is it helping any of us?
- Will I be proud of how I conducted myself in hindsight?
- What can I tell myself that would be more supportive to me now?
- If the main purpose of this situation was for the learning and growth of me, the team, and the business—how would I/we approach it differently?
- If there was a giant opportunity included in this situation, what might it be?
- Since I'm definitely not a wizard, villain, or victim, can I give myself and others a break for being human?
- What assumptions, biases, and judgements can I just drop for my greater good?

Holding onto judgements will keep you stuck in Self-Protective behaviors. Remember, no good thinking, relating, or creating happens while you are in Self-Protection.

Here's the good news about this step:

The process of releasing judgements you hold about yourself, others and the current situation will free you. Choosing non-judgement automatically engages your natural compassion for yourself and everyone involved.

The experience of compassion often includes:

- A sense of unity and oneness, that we're all in it together (whatever the situational context)
- Competition and win-lose drives drop away as win-win becomes extremely important
- A sense of caring and wanting good things for others and self
- A desire to be of service, and be truly interested and curious about others
- A sense of abundance and confidence that you are able to contribute to others
- A heightened sense of trust and psychological safety, allowing you to risk sharing your perspective and creative ideas while supporting others to do the same

Don't underestimate the importance of reaching compassion before taking action, especially if you are experiencing a high degree of negative emotions.

If you're not feeling compassion after Step 4, keep regulating your emotions and releasing judgements. 'A' Players, like yourself, are often the most critical and judgemental toward themselves. Be aware of this, layers of judgement can be quite stealth, and releasing self-judgement is essential to experience compassion.

Step 5: Engage My Secure Self

You will know that you have completed the CcORE Empowerment Process when you feel the inner ease and freedom that accompanies authentic compassion and enables you to engage in a confidence of security within yourself. This connection to your Secure Self is a high-level characteristic for Self-Leadership. Rather than being concerned so much about yourself, you can now focus outward and contribute your best in teamwork. It moves you out of being self-focused, (which causes you to separate from others, and to seek power and control) to being mutually outcome-focused, open, neutral, and curious. Once you are engaged in your Secure Self, you are then able to develop secure relationships with others to develop the psychologically safe environment that is needed to work together as a united team.

The level of innovation created by a team operating together from Self-Leadership is phenomenal. It creates space for greater cooperation and results than any one player can achieve on their own. Being a part of a united team going for shared outcomes is one of the most fulfilling experiences in leadership.

It's also worth noting that a team of leaders who develop the habit of working the CcORE Empowerment Process before making decisions and taking action, perform much better than those who don't. When you do the CcORE Empowerment Process, you clear the negative energy and problematic self-protection that would have otherwise blocked the best creative thinking.

Doing the CcORE Empowerment Process and moving through the steps might feel like a lot of work at first, but with practice will become more automated in your habitual behavior. Taking the time to learn and develop this new leadership habit will pay big dividends well into the future.

You will likely experience discomfort when you're learning Self-Leadership and the CcORE Empowerment Process. Discomfort is good! It means you are moving through change for growth and learning as you per-severe. Staying comfortable is tied to staying with what you know, and doing things differently requires a willingness to stretch yourself and be uncomfortable while you find your way.

As you strengthen the skills you are learning in this journal, you will be able to endure higher levels of discomfort in the face of challenge and change. You will build the emotional endurance needed to perform well in situations that before were too difficult. And your Self-Awareness will keep increasing, allowing you to make the best choices to achieve results, no matter the situation.

Cultivating emotional endurance through habitually utilizing the CcORE Empowerment Process sets you up to be the kind of leader and team that can make difficult decisions in the midst of high complexity, challenge, and change. It will give you the unique flexibility, responsiveness, and staying power that your competition doesn't have, and bring you to a whole new level of operational excellence. These qualities are essential in performing ahead of the curve as a thriving 'A+' Leader.

"We are not perfect. We are human.
But to avoid reacting, we have to recognize our
behavior and take back the control."

—*ANNIE HYMAN PRATT*

Day 11

▶ Were there any times or situations that were challenging, tense, or stressful where you were able to avoid Self-Protective behaviors and return yourself to Self-Leadership? Did you avoid any reactive behaviors that you've done in the past in similar situations?

_____

_____

_____

_____

_____

▶ When challenged, stressed, or tense, what did you do to avoid Self-Protective emotions driving your behavior, and/or how did you return yourself to Self-Leadership? How did you handle getting triggered?

_____

_____

_____

_____

PRACTICING The CcORE Empowerment Process
Transforming Challenge and Stress into Effective Action

▶ Begin by achieving a state of positive self-regulation of your emotions. Then, from this calm, centered place think of a challenging or stressful situation you experienced recently. **What was the situation?**

▶ **Now, let's take a closer look at the intended outcome**: In the situation from above, describe what you were/are intending or hoping to achieve; what were/are you going for?

_____

_____

_____

_____

_____

▶ **Clarify Situation**: What were the relevant facts of the situation? What's true about the situation as it exists right now (even if it's difficult to accept)? What are the opinions, beliefs, and judgements that must be set aside?

_____

_____

_____

_____

_____

▶ **Choose My Impact**: What do you need to "Do Differently" to achieve the intended outcome? What part do you play in getting to the solution? What positive impact do you intend to have on the situation?

_____

_____

_____

_____

_____

_____

▶ **Observe My Thoughts and Feelings**: What is going on for you emotionally in your current experience? Reminder: naming your feelings helps to shift and de-escalate the energy. I encourage you to state out loud for yourself what you are thinking and feeling. (i.e. I feel angry... sad... frustrated... overwhelmed; I think that _____ may happen).

_____

_____

_____

_____

_____

▶ **Release Judgement to Compassion**: Ask yourself some reflective questions to help you recognize and then release any judgements you're holding:

- What is the story I am telling myself about the current situation?
- What am I holding as "good / bad" or "right / wrong" that I can drop?
- Am I feeling strongly that my position is the only way? What if I let all of that go?
- Can I embrace the idea that I don't know how things will turn out, and ultimately, I do not know what is best?

The truth is that there is so much that goes into any given challenge we are facing, and it is all much bigger than we can know in that moment. The freedom comes in releasing judgement and allowing circumstances to unfold.

▶ Can you reframe the situation? Some thoughts to consider... what can I tell myself that would be more supportive? Is there a bigger opportunity hidden in the current challenge?

▶ **Engage My Secure Self**: This step happens naturally after you release judgement to compassion. Engaging Secure Self includes having compassion and care for yourself and others. You will experience the basic truth that we are all just humans doing the best we can in complex and stressful situations.

Notice how engaging your Secure Self frees you to be confident to

share your perspective openly, increases your willingness to hear others opinions, explore curiously, and change your own thinking without fearing a loss of power, authority, or credibility.

▶ What's present for you now? What do you intend to do next regarding this current situation?

Additional Thoughts

"You, as a leader, need to create the conditions for people to do their most courageous thinking and acting."

—*ANNIE HYMAN PRATT*

Day 12

▶ Were there any times or situations that were challenging, tense, or stressful where you were able to avoid Self-Protective behaviors and return yourself to Self-Leadership? Did you avoid any reactive behaviors that you've done in the past in similar situations?

▶ When challenged, stressed, or tense, what did you do to avoid Self-Protective emotions driving your behavior, and/or how did you return yourself to Self-Leadership? How did you handle getting triggered?

PRACTICING The CcORE Empowerment Process

Transforming Challenge and Stress into Effective Action

▶ Begin by achieving a state of positive self-regulation of your emotions. Then, from this calm, centered place think of a challenging or stressful situation you experienced recently. **What was the situation?**

▶ **Now, let's take a closer look at the intended outcome**: In the situation from above, describe what you were/are intending or hoping to achieve; what were/are you going for?

▶ **Clarify Situation**: What were the relevant facts of the situation? What's true about the situation as it exists right now (even if it's difficult to accept)? What are the opinions, beliefs, and judgements that must be set aside?

▶ **Choose My Impact**: What do you need to "Do Differently" to achieve the intended outcome? What part do you play in getting to the solution? What positive impact do you intend to have on the situation?

_____

_____

_____

_____

▶ **Observe My Thoughts and Feelings**: What is going on for you emotionally in your current experience? Reminder: naming your feelings helps to shift and de-escalate the energy. I encourage you to state out loud for yourself what you are thinking and feeling. (i.e. I feel angry... sad... frustrated... overwhelmed; I think that _____ may happen).

_____

_____

_____

_____

_____

▶ **Release Judgement to Compassion**: Ask yourself some reflective questions to help you recognize and then release any judgements you're holding:

- What is the story I am telling myself about the current situation?
- What am I holding as "good / bad" or "right / wrong" that I can drop?
- Am I feeling strongly that my position is the only way? What if I let all of that go?
- Can I embrace the idea that I don't know how things will turn out, and ultimately, I do not know what is best?

The truth is that there is so much that goes into any given challenge we are facing, and it is all much bigger than we can know in that moment. The freedom comes in releasing judgement and allowing circumstances to unfold.

▶ Can you reframe the situation? Some thoughts to consider... what can I tell myself that would be more supportive? Is there a bigger opportunity hidden in the current challenge?

▶ **Engage My Secure Self**: This step happens naturally after you release judgement to compassion. Engaging Secure Self includes having compassion and care for yourself and others. You will experience the basic truth that we are all just humans doing the best we can in complex and stressful situations.

Notice how engaging your Secure Self frees you to be confident to

share your perspective openly, increases your willingness to hear others opinions, explore curiously, and change your own thinking without fearing a loss of power, authority, or credibility.

_____

_____

_____

_____

_____

_____

▶ What's present for you now? What do you intend to do next regarding this current situation?

_____

_____

_____

_____

_____

_____

Additional Thoughts

"When we understand how leadership really works,
then we are less likely to spend time in Self-Protection.
Because when you are in a situation where you have to do
something different, you have to do something
courageous to get yourself up into Self-Leadership;
something very uncomfortable."

—ANNIE HYMAN PRATT

Day 13

▶ Were there any times or situations that were challenging, tense, or stressful where you were able to avoid Self-Protective behaviors and return yourself to Self-Leadership? Did you avoid any reactive behaviors that you've done in the past in similar situations?

▶ When challenged, stressed, or tense, what did you do to avoid Self-Protective emotions driving your behavior, and/or how did you return yourself to Self-Leadership? How did you handle getting triggered?

PRACTICING The CcORE Empowerment Process
Transforming Challenge and Stress into Effective Action

▶ Begin by achieving a state of positive self-regulation of your emotions. Then, from this calm, centered place think of a challenging or stressful situation you experienced recently. **What was the situation?**

▶ **Now, let's take a closer look at the intended outcome**: In the situation from above, describe what you were/are intending or hoping to achieve; what were/are you going for?

_____

_____

_____

_____

_____

_____

▶ **Clarify Situation**: What were the relevant facts of the situation? What's true about the situation as it exists right now (even if it's difficult to accept)? What are the opinions, beliefs, and judgements that must be set aside?

_____

_____

_____

_____

_____

▶ **Choose My Impact**: What do you need to "Do Differently" to achieve the intended outcome? What part do you play in getting to the solution? What positive impact do you intend to have on the situation?

_____

_____

_____

_____

_____

_____

▶ **Observe My Thoughts and Feelings**: What is going on for you emotionally in your current experience? Reminder: naming your feelings helps to shift and de-escalate the energy. I encourage you to state out loud for yourself what you are thinking and feeling. (i.e. I feel angry... sad... frustrated... overwhelmed; I think that _____ may happen).

_____

_____

_____

_____

_____

▶ **Release Judgement to Compassion**: Ask yourself some reflective questions to help you recognize and then release any judgements you're holding:

- What is the story I am telling myself about the current situation?
- What am I holding as "good / bad" or "right / wrong" that I can drop?
- Am I feeling strongly that my position is the only way? What if I let all of that go?
- Can I embrace the idea that I don't know how things will turn out, and ultimately, I do not know what is best?

The truth is that there is so much that goes into any given challenge we are facing, and it is all much bigger than we can know in that moment. The freedom comes in releasing judgement and allowing circumstances to unfold.

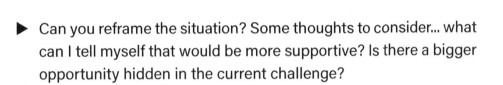

▶ Can you reframe the situation? Some thoughts to consider... what can I tell myself that would be more supportive? Is there a bigger opportunity hidden in the current challenge?

▶ **Engage My Secure Self**: This step happens naturally after you release judgement to compassion. Engaging Secure Self includes having compassion and care for yourself and others. You will experience the basic truth that we are all just humans doing the best we can in complex and stressful situations.

Notice how engaging your Secure Self frees you to be confident to

share your perspective openly, increases your willingness to hear others opinions, explore curiously, and change your own thinking without fearing a loss of power, authority, or credibility.

▶ What's present for you now? What do you intend to do next regarding this current situation?

Additional Thoughts

"Your ability to take action from the Self-Leadership Triangle rides on your ability to withstand discomfort and do something different. The easy way is to fall into Self-Protection; in fact it takes no thought to do—because we are hard-wired to just react."

—ANNIE HYMAN PRATT

Day 14

▶ Were there any times or situations that were challenging, tense, or stressful where you were able to avoid Self-Protective behaviors and return yourself to Self-Leadership? Did you avoid any reactive behaviors that you've done in the past in similar situations?

▶ When challenged, stressed, or tense, what did you do to avoid Self-Protective emotions driving your behavior, and/or how did you return yourself to Self-Leadership? How did you handle getting triggered?

PRACTICING The CcORE Empowerment Process

Transforming Challenge and Stress into Effective Action

Begin by achieving a state of positive self-regulation of your emotions. Then, from this calm, centered place think of a challenging or stressful situation you experienced recently. **What was the situation?**

▶ **Now, let's take a closer look at the intended outcome**: In the situation from above, describe what you were/are intending or hoping to achieve; what were/are you going for?

_____

_____

_____

_____

_____

▶ **Clarify Situation**: What were the relevant facts of the situation? What's true about the situation as it exists right now (even if it's difficult to accept)? What are the opinions, beliefs, and judgements that must be set aside?

_____

_____

_____

_____

_____

▶ **Choose My Impact**: What do you need to "Do Differently" to achieve the intended outcome? What part do you play in getting to the solution? What positive impact do you intend to have on the situation?

_____

_____

_____

_____

_____

_____

▶ **Observe My Thoughts and Feelings**: What is going on for you emotionally in your current experience? Reminder: naming your feelings helps to shift and de-escalate the energy. I encourage you to state out loud for yourself what you are thinking and feeling. (i.e. I feel angry... sad... frustrated... overwhelmed; I think that _____ may happen).

_____

_____

_____

_____

_____

_____

▶ **Release Judgement to Compassion**: Ask yourself some reflective questions to help you recognize and then release any judgements you're holding:

- What is the story I am telling myself about the current situation?
- What am I holding as "good / bad" or "right / wrong" that I can drop?
- Am I feeling strongly that my position is the only way? What if I let all of that go?
- Can I embrace the idea that I don't know how things will turn out, and ultimately, I do not know what is best?

The truth is that there is so much that goes into any given challenge we are facing, and it is all much bigger than we can know in that moment. The freedom comes in releasing judgement and allowing circumstances to unfold.

▶ Can you reframe the situation? Some thoughts to consider... what can I tell myself that would be more supportive? Is there a bigger opportunity hidden in the current challenge?

▶ **Engage My Secure Self**: This step happens naturally after you release judgement to compassion. Engaging Secure Self includes having compassion and care for yourself and others. You will experience the basic truth that we are all just humans doing the best we can in complex and stressful situations.

Notice how engaging your Secure Self frees you to be confident to

share your perspective openly, increases your willingness to hear others opinions, explore curiously, and change your own thinking without fearing a loss of power, authority, or credibility.

▶ What's present for you now? What do you intend to do next regarding this current situation?

"Beginning with a positive intention and staying compassionate really helps guide difficult conversations."

—*ANNIE HYMAN PRATT*

Day 15

▶ Were there any times or situations that were challenging, tense, or stressful where you were able to avoid Self-Protective behaviors and return yourself to Self-Leadership? Did you avoid any reactive behaviors that you've done in the past in similar situations?

▶ When challenged, stressed, or tense, what did you do to avoid Self-Protective emotions driving your behavior, and/or how did you return yourself to Self-Leadership? How did you handle getting triggered?

PRACTICING The CcORE Empowerment Process

Transforming Challenge and Stress into Effective Action

▶ Begin by achieving a state of positive self-regulation of your emotions. Then, from this calm, centered place think of a challenging or stressful situation you experienced recently. **What was the situation?**

_____

_____

_____

_____

_____

▶ **Now, let's take a closer look at the intended outcome**: In the situation from above, describe what you were/are intending or hoping to achieve; what were/are you going for?

_____

_____

_____

_____

_____

_____

▶ **Clarify Situation**: What were the relevant facts of the situation? What's true about the situation as it exists right now (even if it's difficult to accept)? What are the opinions, beliefs, and judgements that must be set aside?

_____

_____

_____

_____

_____

_____

▶ **Choose My Impact**: What do you need to "Do Differently" to achieve the intended outcome? What part do you play in getting to the solution? What positive impact do you intend to have on the situation?

_____

_____

_____

_____

_____

_____

▶ **Observe My Thoughts and Feelings**: What is going on for you emotionally in your current experience? Reminder: naming your feelings helps to shift and de-escalate the energy. I encourage you to state out loud for yourself what you are thinking and feeling. (i.e. I feel angry... sad... frustrated... overwhelmed; I think that _____ may happen).

_____

_____

_____

_____

_____

▶ **Release Judgement to Compassion**: Ask yourself some reflective questions to help you recognize and then release any judgements you're holding:

- What is the story I am telling myself about the current situation?
- What am I holding as "good / bad" or "right / wrong" that I can drop?
- Am I feeling strongly that my position is the only way? What if I let all of that go?
- Can I embrace the idea that I don't know how things will turn out, and ultimately, I do not know what is best?

The truth is that there is so much that goes into any given challenge we are facing, and it is all much bigger than we can know in that moment. The freedom comes in releasing judgement and allowing circumstances to unfold.

▶ Can you reframe the situation? Some thoughts to consider... what can I tell myself that would be more supportive? Is there a bigger opportunity hidden in the current challenge?

▶ **Engage My Secure Self**: This step happens naturally after you release judgement to compassion. Engaging Secure Self includes having compassion and care for yourself and others. You will experience the basic truth that we are all just humans doing the best we can in complex and stressful situations.

Notice how engaging your Secure Self frees you to be confident to

share your perspective openly, increases your willingness to hear others opinions, explore curiously, and change your own thinking without fearing a loss of power, authority, or credibility.

_____

_____

_____

_____

_____

_____

▶ What's present for you now? What do you intend to do next regarding this current situation?

_____

_____

_____

_____

_____

Additional Thoughts

"When you hit system overload, you have two choices: shift up into Self-Leadership or fall into Self-Protection. If you choose Self-Leadership, you can do something productive and take action to get yourself back to a place of effectiveness—otherwise you default to reactive human behavior."

—*ANNIE HYMAN PRATT*

Day 16

▶ Were there any times or situations that were challenging, tense, or stressful where you were able to avoid Self-Protective behaviors and return yourself to Self-Leadership? Did you avoid any reactive behaviors that you've done in the past in similar situations?

_____

_____

_____

_____

_____

▶ When challenged, stressed, or tense, what did you do to avoid Self-Protective emotions driving your behavior, and/or how did you return yourself to Self-Leadership? How did you handle getting triggered?

_____

_____

_____

_____

PRACTICING The CcORE Empowerment Process

Transforming Challenge and Stress into Effective Action

SELF-LEADERSHIP

E Engage
R Release
O Observe
C Choose
C Clarify

™ © 2020 Annie Hyman Pratt | Leading Edge Teams

▶ Begin by achieving a state of positive self-regulation of your emotions. Then, from this calm, centered place think of a challenging or stressful situation you experienced recently. **What was the situation?**

▶ **Now, let's take a closer look at the intended outcome**: In the situation from above, describe what you were/are intending or hoping to achieve; what were/are you going for?

_____

_____

_____

_____

_____

_____

▶ **Clarify Situation**: What were the relevant facts of the situation? What's true about the situation as it exists right now (even if it's difficult to accept)? What are the opinions, beliefs, and judgements that must be set aside?

_____

_____

_____

_____

_____

▶ **Choose My Impact**: What do you need to "Do Differently" to achieve the intended outcome? What part do you play in getting to the solution? What positive impact do you intend to have on the situation?

_____

_____

_____

_____

_____

_____

▶ **Observe My Thoughts and Feelings**: What is going on for you emotionally in your current experience? Reminder: naming your feelings helps to shift and de-escalate the energy. I encourage you to state out loud for yourself what you are thinking and feeling. (i.e. I feel angry... sad... frustrated... overwhelmed; I think that _____ may happen).

_____

_____

_____

_____

_____

▶ **Release Judgement to Compassion**: Ask yourself some reflective questions to help you recognize and then release any judgements you're holding:

- What is the story I am telling myself about the current situation?
- What am I holding as "good / bad" or "right / wrong" that I can drop?
- Am I feeling strongly that my position is the only way? What if I let all of that go?
- Can I embrace the idea that I don't know how things will turn out, and ultimately, I do not know what is best?

The truth is that there is so much that goes into any given challenge we are facing, and it is all much bigger than we can know in that moment. The freedom comes in releasing judgement and allowing circumstances to unfold.

▶ Can you reframe the situation? Some thoughts to consider... what can I tell myself that would be more supportive? Is there a bigger opportunity hidden in the current challenge?

▶ **Engage My Secure Self**: This step happens naturally after you release judgement to compassion. Engaging Secure Self includes having compassion and care for yourself and others. You will experience the basic truth that we are all just humans doing the best we can in complex and stressful situations.

Notice how engaging your Secure Self frees you to be confident to

share your perspective openly, increases your willingness to hear others opinions, explore curiously, and change your own thinking without fearing a loss of power, authority, or credibility.

▶ What's present for you now? What do you intend to do next regarding this current situation?

Additional Thoughts

"One of the biggest mistakes we make is thinking that all behavior is derived from intent."

—*ANNIE HYMAN PRATT*

Day 17

▶ Were there any times or situations that were challenging, tense, or stressful where you were able to avoid Self-Protective behaviors and return yourself to Self-Leadership? Did you avoid any reactive behaviors that you've done in the past in similar situations?

_____

_____

_____

_____

_____

▶ When challenged, stressed, or tense, what did you do to avoid Self-Protective emotions driving your behavior, and/or how did you return yourself to Self-Leadership? How did you handle getting triggered?

_____

_____

_____

_____

PRACTICING The CcORE Empowerment Process

Transforming Challenge and Stress into Effective Action

▶ Begin by achieving a state of positive self-regulation of your emotions. Then, from this calm, centered place think of a challenging or stressful situation you experienced recently. **What was the situation?**

_____
_____
_____
_____
_____

▶ **Now, let's take a closer look at the intended outcome**: In the situation from above, describe what you were/are intending or hoping to achieve; what were/are you going for?

_____

_____

_____

_____

_____

▶ **Clarify Situation**: What were the relevant facts of the situation? What's true about the situation as it exists right now (even if it's difficult to accept)? What are the opinions, beliefs, and judgements that must be set aside?

_____

_____

_____

_____

_____

▶ **Choose My Impact**: What do you need to "Do Differently" to achieve the intended outcome? What part do you play in getting to the solution? What positive impact do you intend to have on the situation?

_____

_____

_____

_____

_____

_____

▶ **Observe My Thoughts and Feelings**: What is going on for you emotionally in your current experience? Reminder: naming your feelings helps to shift and de-escalate the energy. I encourage you to state out loud for yourself what you are thinking and feeling. (i.e. I feel angry... sad... frustrated... overwhelmed; I think that _____ may happen).

_____

_____

_____

_____

_____

_____

▶ **Release Judgement to Compassion**: Ask yourself some reflective questions to help you recognize and then release any judgements you're holding:

- What is the story I am telling myself about the current situation?
- What am I holding as "good / bad" or "right / wrong" that I can drop?
- Am I feeling strongly that my position is the only way? What if I let all of that go?
- Can I embrace the idea that I don't know how things will turn out, and ultimately, I do not know what is best?

The truth is that there is so much that goes into any given challenge we are facing, and it is all much bigger than we can know in that moment. The freedom comes in releasing judgement and allowing circumstances to unfold.

▶ Can you reframe the situation? Some thoughts to consider... what can I tell myself that would be more supportive? Is there a bigger opportunity hidden in the current challenge?

▶ **Engage My Secure Self:** This step happens naturally after you release judgement to compassion. Engaging Secure Self includes having compassion and care for yourself and others. You will experience the basic truth that we are all just humans doing the best we can in complex and stressful situations.

Notice how engaging your Secure Self frees you to be confident to

share your perspective openly, increases your willingness to hear others opinions, explore curiously, and change your own thinking without fearing a loss of power, authority, or credibility.

▶ What's present for you now? What do you intend to do next regarding this current situation?

Additional Thoughts

"We only have control over what we do, and the best we can do is stay in Self-Leadership."

—*ANNIE HYMAN PRATT*

▶▶▶

Day 18

▶ Were there any times or situations that were challenging, tense, or stressful where you were able to avoid Self-Protective behaviors and return yourself to Self-Leadership? Did you avoid any reactive behaviors that you've done in the past in similar situations?

▶ When challenged, stressed, or tense, what did you do to avoid Self-Protective emotions driving your behavior, and/or how did you return yourself to Self-Leadership? How did you handle getting triggered?

PRACTICING The CcORE Empowerment Process

Transforming Challenge and Stress into Effective Action

► Begin by achieving a state of positive self-regulation of your emotions. Then, from this calm, centered place think of a challenging or stressful situation you experienced recently. **What was the situation?**

Annie Hyman Pratt

▶ **Now, let's take a closer look at the intended outcome**: In the situation from above, describe what you were/are intending or hoping to achieve; what were/are you going for?

_____

_____

_____

_____

_____

▶ **Clarify Situation**: What were the relevant facts of the situation? What's true about the situation as it exists right now (even if it's difficult to accept)? What are the opinions, beliefs, and judgements that must be set aside?

_____

_____

_____

_____

_____

▶ **Choose My Impact**: What do you need to "Do Differently" to achieve the intended outcome? What part do you play in getting to the solution? What positive impact do you intend to have on the situation?

_____

_____

_____

_____

_____

_____

▶ **Observe My Thoughts and Feelings**: What is going on for you emotionally in your current experience? Reminder: naming your feelings helps to shift and de-escalate the energy. I encourage you to state out loud for yourself what you are thinking and feeling. (i.e. I feel angry... sad... frustrated... overwhelmed; I think that _____ may happen).

_____

_____

_____

_____

_____

▶ **Release Judgement to Compassion**: Ask yourself some reflective questions to help you recognize and then release any judgements you're holding:

- What is the story I am telling myself about the current situation?
- What am I holding as "good / bad" or "right / wrong" that I can drop?
- Am I feeling strongly that my position is the only way? What if I let all of that go?
- Can I embrace the idea that I don't know how things will turn out, and ultimately, I do not know what is best?

The truth is that there is so much that goes into any given challenge we are facing, and it is all much bigger than we can know in that moment. The freedom comes in releasing judgement and allowing circumstances to unfold.

▶ Can you reframe the situation? Some thoughts to consider... what can I tell myself that would be more supportive? Is there a bigger opportunity hidden in the current challenge?

▶ **Engage My Secure Self**: This step happens naturally after you release judgement to compassion. Engaging Secure Self includes having compassion and care for yourself and others. You will experience the basic truth that we are all just humans doing the best we can in complex and stressful situations.

Notice how engaging your Secure Self frees you to be confident to

share your perspective openly, increases your willingness to hear others opinions, explore curiously, and change your own thinking without fearing a loss of power, authority, or credibility.

▶ What's present for you now? What do you intend to do next regarding this current situation?

"When we work on behavior, and as we grow and develop, our areas of weakness are revealed and sometimes we overcompensate. Don't beat yourself up when you realize this. It's actually a good sign. The great thing about polarity is that often you have to experience the extremes to find your balance."

—*ANNIE HYMAN PRATT*

▶▶▶

Day 19

▶ Were there any times or situations that were challenging, tense, or stressful where you were able to avoid Self-Protective behaviors and return yourself to Self-Leadership? Did you avoid any reactive behaviors that you've done in the past in similar situations?

_____

_____

_____

_____

_____

_____

▶ When challenged, stressed, or tense, what did you do to avoid Self-Protective emotions driving your behavior, and/or how did you return yourself to Self-Leadership? How did you handle getting triggered?

_____

_____

_____

_____

PRACTICING The CcORE Empowerment Process

Transforming Challenge and Stress into Effective Action

SELF-LEADERSHIP

E Engage

R Release

O Observe

C Choose

C Clarify

™ © 2020 Annie Hyman Pratt | Leading Edge Teams

▶ Begin by achieving a state of positive self-regulation of your emotions. Then, from this calm, centered place think of a challenging or stressful situation you experienced recently. **What was the situation?**

▶ **Now, let's take a closer look at the intended outcome**: In the situation from above, describe what you were/are intending or hoping to achieve; what were/are you going for?

_____

_____

_____

_____

_____

▶ **Clarify Situation**: What were the relevant facts of the situation? What's true about the situation as it exists right now (even if it's difficult to accept)? What are the opinions, beliefs, and judgements that must be set aside?

_____

_____

_____

_____

▶ **Choose My Impact**: What do you need to "Do Differently" to achieve the intended outcome? What part do you play in getting to the solution? What positive impact do you intend to have on the situation?

_____

_____

_____
_____
_____
_____

▶ **Observe My Thoughts and Feelings**: What is going on for you emotionally in your current experience? Reminder: naming your feelings helps to shift and de-escalate the energy. I encourage you to state out loud for yourself what you are thinking and feeling. (i.e. I feel angry... sad... frustrated... overwhelmed; I think that _____ may happen).

_____
_____
_____
_____
_____

▶ **Release Judgement to Compassion**: Ask yourself some reflective questions to help you recognize and then release any judgements you're holding:

- What is the story I am telling myself about the current situation?
- What am I holding as "good / bad" or "right / wrong" that I can drop?
- Am I feeling strongly that my position is the only way? What if I let all of that go?
- Can I embrace the idea that I don't know how things will turn out, and ultimately, I do not know what is best?

The truth is that there is so much that goes into any given challenge we are facing, and it is all much bigger than we can know in that moment. The freedom comes in releasing judgement and allowing circumstances to unfold.

▶ Can you reframe the situation? Some thoughts to consider... what can I tell myself that would be more supportive? Is there a bigger opportunity hidden in the current challenge?

▶ **Engage My Secure Self**: This step happens naturally after you release judgement to compassion. Engaging Secure Self includes having compassion and care for yourself and others. You will experience the basic truth that we are all just humans doing the best we can in complex and stressful situations.

Notice how engaging your Secure Self frees you to be confident to

share your perspective openly, increases your willingness to hear others opinions, explore curiously, and change your own thinking without fearing a loss of power, authority, or credibility.

▶ What's present for you now? What do you intend to do next regarding this current situation?

Additional Thoughts

"We all wind up in Self-Protection. The real competency is recognizing it and getting ourselves out."

—*ANNIE HYMAN PRATT*

Day 20

▶ Were there any times or situations that were challenging, tense, or stressful where you were able to avoid Self-Protective behaviors and return yourself to Self-Leadership? Did you avoid any reactive behaviors that you've done in the past in similar situations?

▶ When challenged, stressed, or tense, what did you do to avoid Self-Protective emotions driving your behavior, and/or how did you return yourself to Self-Leadership? How did you handle getting triggered?

PRACTICING The CcORE Empowerment Process

Transforming Challenge and Stress into Effective Action

SELF-LEADERSHIP

E Engage
R Release
O Observe
C Choose
C Clarify

™ © 2020 Annie Hyman Pratt | Leading Edge Teams

▶ Begin by achieving a state of positive self-regulation of your emotions. Then, from this calm, centered place think of a challenging or stressful situation you experienced recently. **What was the situation?**

_____

_____

_____

_____

_____

_____

▶ **Now, let's take a closer look at the intended outcome**: In the situation from above, describe what you were/are intending or hoping to achieve; what were/are you going for?

_____

_____

_____

_____

_____

▶ **Clarify Situation**: What were the relevant facts of the situation? What's true about the situation as it exists right now (even if it's difficult to accept)? What are the opinions, beliefs, and judgements that must be set aside?

_____

_____

_____

_____

▶ **Choose My Impact**: What do you need to "Do Differently" to achieve the intended outcome? What part do you play in getting to the solution? What positive impact do you intend to have on the situation?

_____

_____

_____

_____

_____

_____

▶ **Observe My Thoughts and Feelings**: What is going on for you emotionally in your current experience? Reminder: naming your feelings helps to shift and de-escalate the energy. I encourage you to state out loud for yourself what you are thinking and feeling. (i.e. I feel angry... sad... frustrated... overwhelmed; I think that _____ may happen).

_____

_____

_____

_____

_____

▶ **Release Judgement to Compassion**: Ask yourself some reflective questions to help you recognize and then release any judgements you're holding:

- What is the story I am telling myself about the current situation?
- What am I holding as "good / bad" or "right / wrong" that I can drop?
- Am I feeling strongly that my position is the only way? What if I let all of that go?
- Can I embrace the idea that I don't know how things will turn out, and ultimately, I do not know what is best?

The truth is that there is so much that goes into any given challenge we are facing, and it is all much bigger than we can know in that moment. The freedom comes in releasing judgement and allowing circumstances to unfold.

_____

_____

_____

_____

_____

_____

▶ Can you reframe the situation? Some thoughts to consider... what can I tell myself that would be more supportive? Is there a bigger opportunity hidden in the current challenge?

_____

_____

_____

_____

_____

_____

▶ **Engage My Secure Self**: This step happens naturally after you release judgement to compassion. Engaging Secure Self includes having compassion and care for yourself and others. You will experience the basic truth that we are all just humans doing the best we can in complex and stressful situations.

Notice how engaging your Secure Self frees you to be confident to

share your perspective openly, increases your willingness to hear others opinions, explore curiously, and change your own thinking without fearing a loss of power, authority, or credibility.

▶ What's present for you now? What do you intend to do next regarding this current situation?

20-Day Check-in

Working the CcORE Empowerment Process

SELF-LEADERSHIP

E	**Engage**	Engage My Secure Self
R	**Release**	Release Judgement to Compassion
O	**Observe**	Observe My Thoughts & Feelings
C	**Choose**	Choose My Impact
C	**Clarify**	Clarify Situtation

™ © 2020 Annie Hyman Pratt | Leading Edge Teams

Developing Self-Leadership skills, and your continued practice in the moment as situations unfold, is essential to shift your habits. It will support you to develop the ability to regulate your emotions in increasingly difficult moments of challenge and change. You will be able to navigate a more complex business landscape, while experiencing greater ease. Emotional regulation enables you to anchor in your intended outcomes and address the current situation with empowered choice for the impact you are going for.

▶ What do you now know about yourself and your leadership that you didn't know before?

_____

_____

_____

_____

_____

▶ To what degree have you mastered working the steps of the CcORE Empowerment Process?

_____

_____

_____

_____

_____

▶ Describe what it is like for you when you have released judgements and shifted to the experience of authentic compassion.

_____

_____

_____

_____

▶ When you are engaged in your secure self, how are you thinking and behaving in ways that are having a positive impact on your interactions and collaborations with others? What progress or results are you achieving that you weren't before?

Opportunities and Rapid Change Through Self-Leadership

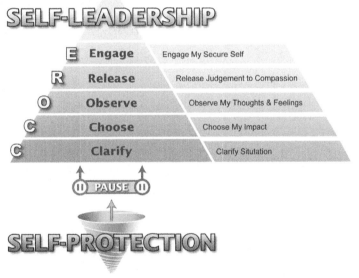

"Be the change that you wish to see in the world."

—*MAHATMA GANDHI*

Lesson 3

If you've been practicing Self-Leadership and self-awareness, you've likely recognized yourself acting from emotional reactivity (Self-Protection) at least a few times, and maybe many times. This is the natural human behavior that is managed through Self-Leadership. We hope you then used the power of the PAUSE, and were able to regulate your emotions and work through the steps of the CcORE Empowerment Process.

These 'A+' Leadership skills are also a huge part of what's traditionally known as emotional intelligence and necessary to navigate your feelings and emotions. Emotional intelligence starts with skills like identifying and naming your feelings and needs, which then enables you to more easily recognize others' feelings and listen with empathy because you've pro-cessed and toned down or let go of your emotions. Becoming competent and confident in these skills is a big part of effective leadership.

Two Areas to Continually Advance in your Self-Leadership:

1) Stealth Self-Protection behaviors
2) Maintaining Self-Leadership when stakes, stress, and pressure increase (aka increasing your Emotional Endurance)

The treachery of the stealth Self-Protection:

Human self-protection behaviors are so ingrained into our habits and everyday lives, that some can be especially hard to detect or identify. But, however hard to detect, these are still worth addressing, because they hold you back from continuing to grow and reaching your potential.

A common example of a stealth Self-Protection habit is taking over-responsibility and self-blame when encountering mistakes and problems. For example, say your team just made a big, costly error, the inner dialogue is usually something like this:

> *"Ugh, this is a big, costly mistake that my team just made, but I should have known that my team wasn't ready to handle that project on their own. I should have anticipated that they'd likely make this mistake. Or I at least should have checked on them way more so that I caught it earlier. So in reality it's really my fault. After all, it is my business so I'm ultimately responsible for everything that happens in it. So I guess I just messed up big-time."*

On the surface this actually looks like a super mature and effective demonstration of leadership, right? The leader above isn't blaming their team, or deflecting the problem, so it seems all good somehow.

But it's NOT. Self-blame is a quickly spiraling, emotionally reactive behavior, just like all the others. Because the consequences of self-blame are dire; much more dire than most people understand.

Imagine yourself in the leader's shoes above, and that you've just told your team that the mistake is not their fault, but it's really yours. Here's the thoughts and feelings that usually happen next, and the resulting behaviors:

Leader thoughts and feelings:

> *"Oh my gosh, my team isn't nearly as capable as I thought and I'm going to have to take back lots of responsibilities that I don't have time for. That makes me feel resentful because*

I've invested a lot in my team and now they can't even do the work that they signed on for. I guess I hired a sub-par team, which I also now need to deal with because I can't afford an unproductive team!

Maybe I'll never find a good enough team, one as good as me, and I'll be stuck forever with too much work. I guess I need to learn how to hire—ugh, it really is all on me. Maybe I'm not cut out for being a business leader. There's just too much I need to learn and not enough time. But, hmm... other leaders can do it, so maybe I'm not as good as I think, and I'm actually doomed for failure? OK, I better push myself way, way harder in every area or I really will fail!"

With those thoughts and feelings, the leader's next actions are most likely to isolate, take back responsibilities, and try to regain confidence by "figuring it out" on his/her own. That usually sounds something like this with the team:

"Hey everyone, thanks for meeting, but I don't think we really need to debrief this mistake. I get what happened and I know what I need to do next. So my time is better spent with me just figuring out the new plan on how to go forward. I'll get back to you all when I have that plan."

This sequence of thoughts and actions will almost certainly lead to the absolute worst results! The team will not contribute important perspective and problem solving ideas. When they lose responsibility, they feel devalued and become much less committed. The leader will take on work that they can't really do, which will lead to more self-criticism and isolation.

The end result is that instead of learning from the mistake and empowering the team to step-up, the leader's self-blame sets off a series of behaviors that cause the whole organization to become less effective and less able to move forward positively—usually resulting in compounding mistakes and more stress and problems.

Another stealth Self-Protection behavior is taking under-responsibility and framing it as giving others autonomy and empowerment to make decisions, but then blaming the team when things go wrong or they don't produce the result.

Let's imagine the same example, where your team just made a big, costly error; the inner dialogue is usually something like this:

> *"Ugh, this is a big, costly mistake that my team just made. This should never have happened and I can't believe they so totally let me down. I gave them such a great opportunity to really go for it, without me getting in the way, and they totally messed up... Ironic that they were saying how I do things is the real problem! I get results when I do things! I guess they're not nearly as good as I thought they were, and not nearly as good as I need them to be."*

Again, on the surface this sounds pretty plausible. Maybe the team isn't competent enough and made a commitment they couldn't keep. After all, it sounds like the leader got out of the way so that the team could work unhindered and without being micromanaged. The team didn't say that they couldn't be counted on to deliver the result, so it does seem like the team is to blame in this example.

But blame in ANY situation is a big problem with enormous negative consequences. This seems rather obvious in most situations that people imagine. It's actually fairly difficult to separate blame from responsibility in a way that makes intuitive sense—that's what makes it a "stealth" reactive behavior.

So imagine yourself in the leader's shoes above and that you've just told your team that the mistake is their fault and that they need to take responsibility for it. Here's the thoughts and feelings that usually happen next and the resulting behaviors:

Typical leader thoughts and feelings:

> *"Oh my gosh, my team just proved what I initially suspected—that they're not competent and capable, and without me they can't get the results. That makes me feel resentful because I've invested a lot in my team and now they can't even do the work that they signed on for. I guess I hired a sub-par team, which I probably need to replace because I can't afford an unproductive team! I'm so disappointed!*
>
> *They must be more capable than I'm giving them credit. Maybe I'm just being too nice and not holding them accountable enough. They must not be motivated to do what's really needed to get results. If I weren't so nice, maybe they'd care more and try way harder. Oh, and they clearly don't know how to prioritize to be more productive. I'll make them use one of those organization systems to fix that.*
>
> *Ultimately, I think I just need to change my style to more "tough love." And my team tells me that we need better systems—so we'll put in some of those too, because that will free their time so they can prioritize.*
>
> *And if this doesn't work, I'll just replace them. There's some great people out there, I just have to find them."*

With those thoughts and feelings, the leader's next actions are most likely to give feedback by making clear what the team did wrong, followed by strong demands for producing the results, and some specifics for what the team should do differently to become more productive and effective. That usually sounds something like this with the team:

"Hey everyone, well I'm sorry to report that this project didn't go well at all. You guys and gals made several mistakes that cost us a lot of money. First there was the email mistake with the wrong link and wrong date/time. Then there was an order taking problem that compounded because we were totally unprepared to handle the swell of angry and confused customers in customer service.

Because of this situation, we're going to have to raise the targeted results for our next project, and add in an additional project to connect with customers. So first thing—to get more organized you're all going to use the new digital project management tool. Second, you're going to share with me each day what you're focusing on, so that I know what you're prioritizing.

Third, the next project has to go extremely well or I won't be able to keep everyone on. I will let you hire one more person, and that should be plenty to achieve the results."

Again, this sequence of thoughts and actions will almost certainly lead to the absolute worst results! This team will feel stressed, threatened, insecure, and, at the same time, resentful of the entrepreneur not taking any meaningful ownership for the poor results. They will also feel that their best next moves are to merely try to do exactly what they're told, and to NOT think on their own. That will lead to them taking less and less responsibility and achieving worse and worse results.

The end result is that instead of learning from the mistake and then everyone bearing mutual responsibility to achieve better results, a self-fulfilling spiral of poorer and poorer performance will ensue with the leader losing all faith in their team and then moving on to find another "better" team.

Other behaviors that are common stealth Self-Protection:

- Pleasing others by saying "yes" when you mean "maybe" or "no"
- Agreeing even if you have a different opinion or perspective
- Clarifying "agreements" while also adding urgency and pressure—so that others have no real choice and must commit (this is a stealth demand)
- Pressing for speed and action even though the situation would benefit much more from thinking and strategizing
- Taking back responsibilities even when others are reasonably capable—to "protect them" from discomfort
- Giving others "space" when they really need connection—so that you can avoid confronting an uncomfortable situation
- Pausing decision-making so that you can "think more," when that thinking won't meaningfully change the decision you'd make now
- Staying overwhelmed or confused is actually a tricky emotionally-driven reaction that leaves you trapped. It leaves you in a place of powerlessness and sets you up to avoid taking more responsibility to influence your task load or clarity (though, of course, that is not your conscious intent)

Something we rarely think about in leadership, let alone in Self-Leadership, is that things gets exponentially more difficult when the stakes, pressure, or stress, increases. It definitely makes sense when you think about it, because in those situations we're supposed to be Self-Protective! Right?

Well... no. Context matters here. When humans were developing, the stakes, stress and pressure was surrounding issues of survival. They developed these hard-wired behaviors to preserve their lives.

But in most of the modern world today, especially in the modern business world, we no longer need to worry about our survival. Only a teeny-tiny fraction of business problems result in death and those usually follow highly dangerous endeavors, like building a sky-scraper.

The problem is the stress FEELS the same, with the same emotions and urges getting triggered to put us into reactive Self-Protection. But those reactive behaviors are the opposite of what's needed to work through business stress, pressure and high stakes issues!

As you improve in leadership, taking on higher-level responsibilities that naturally include more stress, pressure, and high-stakes, your ability to maintain your Self-Leadership becomes more and more important. Having the needed functional skills matters; however, you won't get to utilize them properly if you're in a reactive behavior spiral.

THIS IS A PRACTICE

We think of Self-Leadership as an ongoing practice, one that you continually improve to positively impact all areas of your performance. In the same way that we build our athleticism and physical endurance when seeking growth, improvement, and mastery in sports, we need to build our Self-Leadership and emotional endurance in order to grow, improve, and excel in leadership, teamwork, and business!

As you continue to practice your new habit of approaching business interactions from the CcORE Empowerment Process, you'll experience many positive impacts. One being a higher degree of psychological safety for all who interact with you as you maintain yourself as a blame-free zone. Your team will notice you shift away from conflict and towards neutrality, inclusion, and openness. You'll look at issues from multiple perspectives and welcome collaboration which leads to better decisions. Others will follow your lead as you demonstrate Self-Leadership in stressful or chaotic situations, while performing at a strong level. And strengthening the emotional endurance of yourself and your team sets the stage for accomplishing ever greater outcomes together.

The best leaders account for the fact that we are humans doing business together, not robots. Our basic needs and feelings are universal. Connecting to the humanity in one another, compassionately, gives us the ability to bring out the best in each other and support one another in regulating our emotions and engaging our Secure Self. From here, everyone thinks, creates, and acts more effectively to resolve issues; including more collaborative engagement of alternative ideas and creative solutions. The best leaders do all this while also moving through the uncertainty and complexity of change that is ever present today.

What we know for sure is that when you strengthen your emotional endurance and develop the new default habit of approaching leadership through the CcORE Empowerment Process, your experience of business and the impact you can have will be transformed. You and your team will be empowered to look ahead, consider options that will shape the future, and guide the business towards even greater opportunities. This is what is meant in the phrase "ahead of the curve" of change. Being "ahead of the curve" empowers you to be a team of innovation and expansion.

Begin this practice today. The next time you are challenged, ask yourself, "What is the greater opportunity hidden in this challenge?"—get your team engaged in answering this question with you and you will achieve extraordinary things and fulfill the "why" that brought you into business in the first place.

"If we move away from the traditional paradigm of authority and control, then we can move toward agreement, alignment, and effective action."

—*ANNIE HYMAN PRATT*

Day 21

▶ Were there any challenges, stress or tense situations that were resolved on the surface, but you realize that there's still some underlying, unresolved issue. If so, what are they?

_____

_____

_____

_____

_____

▶ Was there, or is there, any greater opportunities that surfaced from a challenge, stress or tension that were positive for the business, leadership, teamwork, or relationship growth? Were you happy that an issue surfaced because of what came out of it?

_____

_____

_____

_____

_____

► If so what is that greater opportunity? What are you hoping to achieve?

_____

_____

_____

_____

_____

The CcORE Empowerment Process
Transforming Challenge and Stress into Effective Action

Intended Outcome from the Greater Opportunity:

► **Clarify Situation**: What were the relevant facts of the situation? What's true about the situation as it exists right now (even if it's difficult to accept)? What are the opinions, beliefs, and judgements that must be set aside?

_____

_____

_____

_____

_____

_____

▶ **Choose My Impact**: What do you need to "Do Differently" to achieve the intended outcome? What part do you play in getting to the solution? What positive impact do you intend to have on the situation?

_____

_____

_____

_____

_____

▶ **Observe My Thoughts and Feelings**: What is going on for you emotionally in your current experience? Reminder: naming your feelings helps to shift and de-escalate the energy. I encourage you to state out loud for yourself what you are thinking and feeling (i.e. I feel angry... sad... frustrated... overwhelmed... ; I think that_____may happen).

_____

_____

_____

_____

_____

▶ **Release Judgement to Compassion:**

Ask yourself some reflective questions to help you recognize and then release any judgements you're holding:

- What is the story I am telling myself about the current situation?
- What am I holding as "good / bad" or "right / wrong" that I can drop?
- Am I feeling strongly that my position is the only way? What if I let all of that go?
- Can I embrace the idea that I don't know how things will turn out, and ultimately, I do not know what is best?

The truth is there is so much that goes into any given challenge we are facing and it is all much bigger than we can know in that moment. The freedom comes in releasing judgement and allowing circumstances to unfold.

▶ Can you reframe the situation? Some thoughts to consider... what can I tell myself that would be more supportive? Is there a bigger opportunity hidden in the current challenge?

▶ **Engage My Secure Self**: This step happens naturally after you release judgement. Compassion includes having care and concern for yourself and others. You will experience the basic truth that we are all just humans doing the best we can in complex and stressful situations.

Notice how authentic compassion frees you to share your perspective openly, increases your willingness to hear others opinions, explore curiously and change your own thinking without fearing a loss of power, authority or credibility.

▶ What's present for you now? What do you intend to do next regarding this current situation?

"What we want people doing in our organizations, and as a team, is taking action consistent with an outcome and keeping that in mind constantly, so that we are doing the thing that most empowers the outcome."

—ANNIE HYMAN PRATT

Day 22

▶ Were there any challenges, stress or tense situations that were resolved on the surface, but you realize that there's still some underlying, unresolved issue. If so, what are they?

▶ Was there, or is there, any greater opportunities that surfaced from a challenge, stress or tension that were positive for the business, leadership, teamwork, or relationship growth? Were you happy that an issue surfaced because of what came out of it?

▶ If so what is that greater opportunity? What are you hoping to achieve?

_____

_____

_____

_____

_____

The CcORE Empowerment Process
Transforming Challenge and Stress into Effective Action

Intended Outcome from the Greater Opportunity:

▶ **Clarify Situation**: What were the relevant facts of the situation? What's true about the situation as it exists right now (even if it's difficult to accept)? What are the opinions, beliefs, and judgements that must be set aside?

_____

_____

_____

_____

_____

_____

▶ **Choose My Impact**: What do you need to "Do Differently" to achieve the intended outcome? What part do you play in getting to the solution? What positive impact do you intend to have on the situation?

_____

_____

_____

_____

_____

▶ **Observe My Thoughts and Feelings**: What is going on for you emotionally in your current experience? Reminder: naming your feelings helps to shift and de-escalate the energy. I encourage you to state out loud for yourself what you are thinking and feeling (i.e. I feel angry... sad... frustrated... overwhelmed... ; I think that_____may happen).

_____

_____

_____

▶ **Release Judgement to Compassion:**

Ask yourself some reflective questions to help you recognize and then release any judgements you're holding:

- What is the story I am telling myself about the current situation?
- What am I holding as "good / bad" or "right / wrong" that I can drop?
- Am I feeling strongly that my position is the only way? What if I let all of that go?
- Can I embrace the idea that I don't know how things will turn out, and ultimately, I do not know what is best?

The truth is there is so much that goes into any given challenge we are facing and it is all much bigger than we can know in that moment. The freedom comes in releasing judgement and allowing circumstances to unfold.

_____

_____

_____

_____

▶ Can you reframe the situation? Some thoughts to consider... what can I tell myself that would be more supportive? Is there a bigger opportunity hidden in the current challenge?

_____

_____

_____

_____

▶ **Engage My Secure Self**: This step happens naturally after you release judgement. Compassion includes having care and concern for yourself and others. You will experience the basic truth that we are all just humans doing the best we can in complex and stressful situations.

Notice how authentic compassion frees you to share your perspective openly, increases your willingness to hear others opinions, explore curiously and change your own thinking without fearing a loss of power, authority or credibility.

▶ What's present for you now? What do you intend to do next regarding this current situation?

"You cannot wait to act until you feel better, because the only way to feel better is to act."

—*ANNIE HYMAN PRATT*

Day 23

▶ Were there any challenges, stress or tense situations that were resolved on the surface, but you realize that there's still some underlying, unresolved issue. If so, what are they?

_____

_____

_____

_____

_____

_____

▶ Was there, or is there, any greater opportunities that surfaced from a challenge, stress or tension that were positive for the business, leadership, teamwork, or relationship growth? Were you happy that an issue surfaced because of what came out of it?

_____

_____

_____

_____

_____

▶ If so what is that greater opportunity? What are you hoping to achieve?

_____

_____

_____

_____

_____

The CcORE Empowerment Process
Transforming Challenge and Stress into Effective Action

Intended Outcome from the Greater Opportunity:

▶ **Clarify Situation**: What were the relevant facts of the situation? What's true about the situation as it exists right now (even if it's difficult to accept)? What are the opinions, beliefs, and judgements that must be set aside?

_____

_____

_____

_____

_____

_____

▶ **Choose My Impact:** What do you need to "Do Differently" to achieve the intended outcome? What part do you play in getting to the solution? What positive impact do you intend to have on the situation?

_____

_____

_____

_____

▶ **Observe My Thoughts and Feelings:** What is going on for you emotionally in your current experience? Reminder: naming your feelings helps to shift and de-escalate the energy. I encourage you to state out loud for yourself what you are thinking and feeling (i.e. I feel angry... sad... frustrated... overwhelmed... ; I think that_____may happen).

_____

_____

_____

_____

► **Release Judgement to Compassion**:

Ask yourself some reflective questions to help you recognize and then release any judgements you're holding:

- What is the story I am telling myself about the current situation?
- What am I holding as "good / bad" or "right / wrong" that I can drop?
- Am I feeling strongly that my position is the only way? What if I let all of that go?
- Can I embrace the idea that I don't know how things will turn out, and ultimately, I do not know what is best?

The truth is there is so much that goes into any given challenge we are facing and it is all much bigger than we can know in that moment. The freedom comes in releasing judgement and allowing circumstances to unfold.

► Can you reframe the situation? Some thoughts to consider... what can I tell myself that would be more supportive? Is there a bigger opportunity hidden in the current challenge?

▶ **Engage My Secure Self**: This step happens naturally after you release judgement. Compassion includes having care and concern for yourself and others. You will experience the basic truth that we are all just humans doing the best we can in complex and stressful situations.

Notice how authentic compassion frees you to share your perspective openly, increases your willingness to hear others opinions, explore curiously and change your own thinking without fearing a loss of power, authority or credibility.

▶ What's present for you now? What do you intend to do next regarding this current situation?

"What is Leadership Excellence? A working environment where people can count on each other to take action consistent with agreed upon intended outcomes."

—*ANNIE HYMAN PRATT*

▶▶▶

Day 24

▶ Were there any challenges, stress or tense situations that were resolved on the surface, but you realize that there's still some underlying, unresolved issue. If so, what are they?

_____

_____

_____

_____

_____

_____

▶ Was there, or is there, any greater opportunities that surfaced from a challenge, stress or tension that were positive for the business, leadership, teamwork, or relationship growth? Were you happy that an issue surfaced because of what came out of it?

_____

_____

_____

_____

_____

► If so what is that greater opportunity? What are you hoping to achieve?

_____

_____

_____

_____

_____

The CcORE Empowerment Process
Transforming Challenge and Stress into Effective Action

Intended Outcome from the Greater Opportunity:

► **Clarify Situation**: What were the relevant facts of the situation? What's true about the situation as it exists right now (even if it's difficult to accept)? What are the opinions, beliefs, and judgements that must be set aside?

_____

_____

_____

_____

_____

_____

▶ **Choose My Impact**: What do you need to "Do Differently" to achieve the intended outcome? What part do you play in getting to the solution? What positive impact do you intend to have on the situation?

_____

_____

_____

_____

_____

▶ **Observe My Thoughts and Feelings**: What is going on for you emotionally in your current experience? Reminder: naming your feelings helps to shift and de-escalate the energy. I encourage you to state out loud for yourself what you are thinking and feeling (i.e. I feel angry... sad... frustrated... overwhelmed... ; I think that_____may happen).

_____

_____

_____

_____

► **Release Judgement to Compassion**:

Ask yourself some reflective questions to help you recognize and then release any judgements you're holding:

- What is the story I am telling myself about the current situation?
- What am I holding as "good / bad" or "right / wrong" that I can drop?
- Am I feeling strongly that my position is the only way? What if I let all of that go?
- Can I embrace the idea that I don't know how things will turn out, and ultimately, I do not know what is best?

The truth is there is so much that goes into any given challenge we are facing and it is all much bigger than we can know in that moment. The freedom comes in releasing judgement and allowing circumstances to unfold.

_____

_____

_____

_____

► Can you reframe the situation? Some thoughts to consider... what can I tell myself that would be more supportive? Is there a bigger opportunity hidden in the current challenge?

_____

_____

_____

_____

▶ **Engage My Secure Self**: This step happens naturally after you release judgement. Compassion includes having care and concern for yourself and others. You will experience the basic truth that we are all just humans doing the best we can in complex and stressful situations.

Notice how authentic compassion frees you to share your perspective openly, increases your willingness to hear others opinions, explore curiously and change your own thinking without fearing a loss of power, authority or credibility.

▶ What's present for you now? What do you intend to do next regarding this current situation?

"As we go on, competencies transform into habits.
They run automatically."

—*ANNIE HYMAN PRATT*

Day 25

▶ Were there any challenges, stress or tense situations that were resolved on the surface, but you realize that there's still some underlying, unresolved issue. If so, what are they?

▶ Was there, or is there, any greater opportunities that surfaced from a challenge, stress or tension that were positive for the business, leadership, teamwork, or relationship growth? Were you happy that an issue surfaced because of what came out of it?

▶ If so what is that greater opportunity? What are you hoping to achieve?

_____

_____

_____

_____

_____

_____

The CcORE Empowerment Process
Transforming Challenge and Stress into Effective Action

Intended Outcome from the Greater Opportunity:

▶ **Clarify Situation**: What were the relevant facts of the situation? What's true about the situation as it exists right now (even if it's difficult to accept)? What are the opinions, beliefs, and judgements that must be set aside?

_____

_____

_____

_____

_____

_____

▶ **Choose My Impact**: What do you need to "Do Differently" to achieve the intended outcome? What part do you play in getting to the solution? What positive impact do you intend to have on the situation?

_____

_____

_____

_____

_____

▶ **Observe My Thoughts and Feelings**: What is going on for you emotionally in your current experience? Reminder: naming your feelings helps to shift and de-escalate the energy. I encourage you to state out loud for yourself what you are thinking and feeling (i.e. I feel angry... sad... frustrated... overwhelmed... ; I think that_____may happen).

_____

_____

_____

_____

▶ **Release Judgement to Compassion**:

Ask yourself some reflective questions to help you recognize and then release any judgements you're holding:

- What is the story I am telling myself about the current situation?
- What am I holding as "good / bad" or "right / wrong" that I can drop?
- Am I feeling strongly that my position is the only way? What if I let all of that go?
- Can I embrace the idea that I don't know how things will turn out, and ultimately, I do not know what is best?

The truth is there is so much that goes into any given challenge we are facing and it is all much bigger than we can know in that moment. The freedom comes in releasing judgement and allowing circumstances to unfold.

_____

_____

_____

_____

▶ Can you reframe the situation? Some thoughts to consider... what can I tell myself that would be more supportive? Is there a bigger opportunity hidden in the current challenge?

_____

_____

_____

_____

Annie Hyman Pratt

▶ **Engage My Secure Self**: This step happens naturally after you release judgement. Compassion includes having care and concern for yourself and others. You will experience the basic truth that we are all just humans doing the best we can in complex and stressful situations.

Notice how authentic compassion frees you to share your perspective openly, increases your willingness to hear others opinions, explore curiously and change your own thinking without fearing a loss of power, authority or credibility.

▶ What's present for you now? What do you intend to do next regarding this current situation?

"The more control you exert over your team, the more that your team is dependent on you. And when your team is completely dependent on you, you become a slave to your business."

—*ANNIE HYMAN PRATT*

▶▶▶

Day 26

▶ Were there any challenges, stress or tense situations that were resolved on the surface, but you realize that there's still some underlying, unresolved issue. If so, what are they?

_____

_____

_____

_____

_____

_____

▶ Was there, or is there, any greater opportunities that surfaced from a challenge, stress or tension that were positive for the business, leadership, teamwork, or relationship growth? Were you happy that an issue surfaced because of what came out of it?

_____

_____

_____

_____

_____

► If so what is that greater opportunity? What are you hoping to achieve?

_____

_____

_____

_____

_____

The CcORE Empowerment Process

Transforming Challenge and Stress into Effective Action

Intended Outcome from the Greater Opportunity:

► **Clarify Situation**: What were the relevant facts of the situation? What's true about the situation as it exists right now (even if it's difficult to accept)? What are the opinions, beliefs, and judgements that must be set aside?

_____

_____

_____

_____

_____

_____

▶ **Choose My Impact**: What do you need to "Do Differently" to achieve the intended outcome? What part do you play in getting to the solution? What positive impact do you intend to have on the situation?

_____

_____

_____

_____

_____

▶ **Observe My Thoughts and Feelings**: What is going on for you emotionally in your current experience? Reminder: naming your feelings helps to shift and de-escalate the energy. I encourage you to state out loud for yourself what you are thinking and feeling (i.e. I feel angry... sad... frustrated... overwhelmed... ; I think that_____may happen).

_____

_____

_____

_____

_____

▶ **Release Judgement to Compassion:**

Ask yourself some reflective questions to help you recognize and then release any judgements you're holding:

- What is the story I am telling myself about the current situation?
- What am I holding as "good / bad" or "right / wrong" that I can drop?
- Am I feeling strongly that my position is the only way? What if I let all of that go?
- Can I embrace the idea that I don't know how things will turn out, and ultimately, I do not know what is best?

The truth is there is so much that goes into any given challenge we are facing and it is all much bigger than we can know in that moment. The freedom comes in releasing judgement and allowing circumstances to unfold.

▶ Can you reframe the situation? Some thoughts to consider... what can I tell myself that would be more supportive? Is there a bigger opportunity hidden in the current challenge?

_____

_____

▶ **Engage My Secure Self**: This step happens naturally after you release judgement. Compassion includes having care and concern for yourself and others. You will experience the basic truth that we are all just humans doing the best we can in complex and stressful situations.

Notice how authentic compassion frees you to share your perspective openly, increases your willingness to hear others opinions, explore curiously and change your own thinking without fearing a loss of power, authority or credibility.

_____

_____

_____

_____

_____

▶ What's present for you now? What do you intend to do next regarding this current situation?

_____

_____

_____

_____

_____

"Business is not easy… If you're playing college level sports, you never think 'maybe the other team is going to be really easy on us today.' This is business and no matter what, there's always going to be a feeling of 'we could be doing better.' What I don't want it to turn into is a judgement of how you've done up until now."

—ANNIE HYMAN PRATT

Day 27

▶ Were there any challenges, stress or tense situations that were resolved on the surface, but you realize that there's still some underlying, unresolved issue. If so, what are they?

▶ Was there, or is there, any greater opportunities that surfaced from a challenge, stress or tension that were positive for the business, leadership, teamwork, or relationship growth? Were you happy that an issue surfaced because of what came out of it?

▶ If so what is that greater opportunity? What are you hoping to achieve?

_____

_____

_____

_____

_____

The CcORE Empowerment Process
Transforming Challenge and Stress into Effective Action

Intended Outcome from the Greater Opportunity:

▶ **Clarify Situation**: What were the relevant facts of the situation? What's true about the situation as it exists right now (even if it's difficult to accept)? What are the opinions, beliefs, and judgements that must be set aside?

_____

_____

_____

_____

_____

_____

▶ **Choose My Impact**: What do you need to "Do Differently" to achieve the intended outcome? What part do you play in getting to the solution? What positive impact do you intend to have on the situation?

_____

_____

_____

_____

_____

▶ **Observe My Thoughts and Feelings**: What is going on for you emotionally in your current experience? Reminder: naming your feelings helps to shift and de-escalate the energy. I encourage you to state out loud for yourself what you are thinking and feeling (i.e. I feel angry... sad... frustrated... overwhelmed... ; I think that_____may happen).

_____

_____

_____

_____

▶ Release Judgement to Compassion:

Ask yourself some reflective questions to help you recognize and then release any judgements you're holding:

- What is the story I am telling myself about the current situation?
- What am I holding as "good / bad" or "right / wrong" that I can drop?
- Am I feeling strongly that my position is the only way? What if I let all of that go?
- Can I embrace the idea that I don't know how things will turn out, and ultimately, I do not know what is best?

The truth is there is so much that goes into any given challenge we are facing and it is all much bigger than we can know in that moment. The freedom comes in releasing judgement and allowing circumstances to unfold.

▶ Can you reframe the situation? Some thoughts to consider... what can I tell myself that would be more supportive? Is there a bigger opportunity hidden in the current challenge?

▶ **Engage My Secure Self**: This step happens naturally after you release judgement. Compassion includes having care and concern for yourself and others. You will experience the basic truth that we are all just humans doing the best we can in complex and stressful situations.

Notice how authentic compassion frees you to share your perspective openly, increases your willingness to hear others opinions, explore curiously and change your own thinking without fearing a loss of power, authority or credibility.

▶ What's present for you now? What do you intend to do next regarding this current situation?

"Renegotiation is a generous gift."

—ANNIE HYMAN PRATT

Day 28

▶ Were there any challenges, stress or tense situations that were resolved on the surface, but you realize that there's still some underlying, unresolved issue. If so, what are they?

_____

_____

_____

_____

_____

▶ Was there, or is there, any greater opportunities that surfaced from a challenge, stress or tension that were positive for the business, leadership, teamwork, or relationship growth? Were you happy that an issue surfaced because of what came out of it?

_____

_____

_____

_____

▶ If so what is that greater opportunity? What are you hoping to achieve?

_____

_____

_____

_____

_____

The CcORE Empowerment Process

Transforming Challenge and Stress into Effective Action

Intended Outcome from the Greater Opportunity:

▶ **Clarify Situation**: What were the relevant facts of the situation? What's true about the situation as it exists right now (even if it's difficult to accept)? What are the opinions, beliefs, and judgements that must be set aside?

_____

_____

_____

_____

_____

_____

▶ **Choose My Impact**: What do you need to "Do Differently" to achieve the intended outcome? What part do you play in getting to the solution? What positive impact do you intend to have on the situation?

_____

_____

_____

_____

_____

▶ **Observe My Thoughts and Feelings**: What is going on for you emotionally in your current experience? Reminder: naming your feelings helps to shift and de-escalate the energy. I encourage you to state out loud for yourself what you are thinking and feeling (i.e. I feel angry... sad... frustrated... overwhelmed... ; I think that_____may happen).

_____

_____

_____

_____

▶ Release Judgement to Compassion:

Ask yourself some reflective questions to help you recognize and then release any judgements you're holding:

- What is the story I am telling myself about the current situation?
- What am I holding as "good / bad" or "right / wrong" that I can drop?
- Am I feeling strongly that my position is the only way? What if I let all of that go?
- Can I embrace the idea that I don't know how things will turn out, and ultimately, I do not know what is best?

The truth is there is so much that goes into any given challenge we are facing and it is all much bigger than we can know in that moment. The freedom comes in releasing judgement and allowing circumstances to unfold.

▶ Can you reframe the situation? Some thoughts to consider... what can I tell myself that would be more supportive? Is there a bigger opportunity hidden in the current challenge?

▶ **Engage My Secure Self**: This step happens naturally after you release judgement. Compassion includes having care and concern for yourself and others. You will experience the basic truth that we are all just humans doing the best we can in complex and stressful situations.

Notice how authentic compassion frees you to share your perspective openly, increases your willingness to hear others opinions, explore curiously and change your own thinking without fearing a loss of power, authority or credibility.

▶ What's present for you now? What do you intend to do next regarding this current situation?

"What I've recognized—because I've seen it in myself and so many others—is that we get too responsible for delivering on the big promise. When things aren't going according to plan, you remain in self-blame and blaming others. That's when you're toast!"

—*ANNIE HYMAN PRATT*

Day 29

▶ Were there any challenges, stress or tense situations that were resolved on the surface, but you realize that there's still some underlying, unresolved issue. If so, what are they?

_____

_____

_____

_____

_____

▶ Was there, or is there, any greater opportunities that surfaced from a challenge, stress or tension that were positive for the business, leadership, teamwork, or relationship growth? Were you happy that an issue surfaced because of what came out of it?

_____

_____

_____

_____

▶ If so what is that greater opportunity? What are you hoping to achieve?

_____

_____

_____

_____

_____

_____

The CcORE Empowerment Process
Transforming Challenge and Stress into Effective Action

Intended Outcome from the Greater Opportunity:

▶ **Clarify Situation**: What were the relevant facts of the situation? What's true about the situation as it exists right now (even if it's difficult to accept)? What are the opinions, beliefs, and judgements that must be set aside?

_____

_____

Annie Hyman Pratt

▶ **Choose My Impact**: What do you need to "Do Differently" to achieve the intended outcome? What part do you play in getting to the solution? What positive impact do you intend to have on the situation?

_____

_____

_____

_____

_____

▶ **Observe My Thoughts and Feelings**: What is going on for you emotionally in your current experience? Reminder: naming your feelings helps to shift and de-escalate the energy. I encourage you to state out loud for yourself what you are thinking and feeling (i.e. I feel angry... sad... frustrated... overwhelmed... ; I think that_____may happen).

_____

_____

_____

_____

▶ **Release Judgement to Compassion:**

Ask yourself some reflective questions to help you recognize and then release any judgements you're holding:

- What is the story I am telling myself about the current situation?
- What am I holding as "good / bad" or "right / wrong" that I can drop?
- Am I feeling strongly that my position is the only way? What if I let all of that go?
- Can I embrace the idea that I don't know how things will turn out, and ultimately, I do not know what is best?

The truth is there is so much that goes into any given challenge we are facing and it is all much bigger than we can know in that moment. The freedom comes in releasing judgement and allowing circumstances to unfold.

▶ Can you reframe the situation? Some thoughts to consider... what can I tell myself that would be more supportive? Is there a bigger opportunity hidden in the current challenge?

▶ **Engage My Secure Self**: This step happens naturally after you release judgement. Compassion includes having care and concern for yourself and others. You will experience the basic truth that we are all just humans doing the best we can in complex and stressful situations.

Notice how authentic compassion frees you to share your perspective openly, increases your willingness to hear others opinions, explore curiously and change your own thinking without fearing a loss of power, authority or credibility.

▶ What's present for you now? What do you intend to do next regarding this current situation?

"You don't know what you don't know yet.
We all have blind spots."

—*ANNIE HYMAN PRATT*

Day 30

▶ Were there any challenges, stress or tense situations that were resolved on the surface, but you realize that there's still some underlying, unresolved issue. If so, what are they?

_____

_____

_____

_____

_____

_____

▶ Was there, or is there, any greater opportunities that surfaced from a challenge, stress or tension that were positive for the business, leadership, teamwork, or relationship growth? Were you happy that an issue surfaced because of what came out of it?

_____

_____

_____

_____

_____

▶ If so what is that greater opportunity? What are you hoping to achieve?

_____

_____

_____

_____

_____

The CcORE Empowerment Process
Transforming Challenge and Stress into Effective Action

Intended Outcome from the Greater Opportunity:

▶ **Clarify Situation**: What were the relevant facts of the situation? What's true about the situation as it exists right now (even if it's difficult to accept)? What are the opinions, beliefs, and judgements that must be set aside?

_____

_____

_____

_____

_____

_____

_____

▶ **Choose My Impact**: What do you need to "Do Differently" to achieve the intended outcome? What part do you play in getting to the solution? What positive impact do you intend to have on the situation?

_____

_____

_____

_____

_____

▶ **Observe My Thoughts and Feelings**: What is going on for you emotionally in your current experience? Reminder: naming your feelings helps to shift and de-escalate the energy. I encourage you to state out loud for yourself what you are thinking and feeling (i.e. I feel angry... sad... frustrated... overwhelmed... ; I think that_____may happen).

_____

_____

_____

_____

► **Release Judgement to Compassion**:

Ask yourself some reflective questions to help you recognize and then release any judgements you're holding:

- What is the story I am telling myself about the current situation?
- What am I holding as "good / bad" or "right / wrong" that I can drop?
- Am I feeling strongly that my position is the only way? What if I let all of that go?
- Can I embrace the idea that I don't know how things will turn out, and ultimately, I do not know what is best?

The truth is there is so much that goes into any given challenge we are facing and it is all much bigger than we can know in that moment. The freedom comes in releasing judgement and allowing circumstances to unfold.

► Can you reframe the situation? Some thoughts to consider... what can I tell myself that would be more supportive? Is there a bigger opportunity hidden in the current challenge?

▶ **Engage My Secure Self**: This step happens naturally after you release judgement. Compassion includes having care and concern for yourself and others. You will experience the basic truth that we are all just humans doing the best we can in complex and stressful situations.

Notice how authentic compassion frees you to share your perspective openly, increases your willingness to hear others opinions, explore curiously and change your own thinking without fearing a loss of power, authority or credibility.

▶ What's present for you now? What do you intend to do next regarding this current situation?

Additional Thoughts

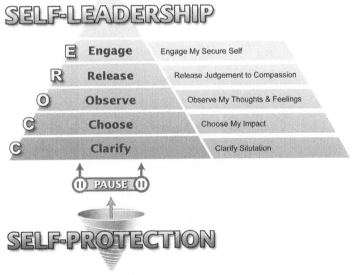

30-Day Check-in

Opportunities and Rapid Change via the Self-Leadership Habit

SELF-LEADERSHIP

E	**Engage**	Engage My Secure Self
R	**Release**	Release Judgement to Compassion
O	**Observe**	Observe My Thoughts & Feelings
C	**Choose**	Choose My Impact
C	**Clarify**	Clarify Situation

PAUSE

SELF-PROTECTION

™ © 2020 Annie Hyman Pratt | Leading Edge Teams

Congratulations! You have completed your 30-Day journey of exploring and developing your Self-Leadership. Acknowledgement is a positive way to secure your new habits and reward your commitment to strengthen your leadership.

Take a moment now to review and acknowledge your progress and success:

My 30-Day Results

▶ Why were you interested in growing your leadership (with self and others)? Refer to Pages 7–9 in this journal: Did you achieve growth in those areas? What changed?

_____

_____

_____

_____

_____

▶ Have you improved your leadership in the areas where you were challenged? If so, what were the improvements?

_____

_____

_____

_____

_____

▶ What were your 30-day goals for this process? Did you achieve those?

_____

_____

_____

_____

_____

_____

▶ What are you doing differently in your leadership now?

_____

_____

_____

_____

_____

_____

And Now Your Leadership Journey Continues…

Now that you've experienced the growth of the past 30 days, what's next for your leadership development?

▶ Advanced Self-Leadership: Do you see any areas where increasing your Self-Leadership and Emotional Endurance would more greatly benefit you, your team, and your company?

_____

_____

▶ Advanced Agreement Making: What agreements could you create with your team that would increase psychological safety? How could you develop higher levels of critical thinking and problem solving together?

▶ Advanced Leadership: Knowing there are even greater opportunities available, what intentions would you like to set to further learn and grow in your leadership?

Congratulations

Our wish for you…

Now that you have achieved these new habits of Self-Leadership, we celebrate your dedication to this process. The journey of business today is not a straight line from A (where you are now) to V (achieving the vision of your future desired state), but with your new skill of shifting out of emotional reactivity you have what it takes to ride out the peaks and valleys, and enjoy the process of achieving your goals and success. Our wish for you is that you continue to practice and strengthen these habits, while learning more of the essentials of Leadership Mastery.

To support your continued success, we invite you to go to **https://leadingedgeteams.com/introduction-agreements** and download a Bonus Gift for you:

This **Bonus Gift** for you is an **Introduction to AGREEMENTS**.

In business, agreements are your main mechanism for working together, as they are the foundational way that you interact to make commitments to do "your part" of any function, project, or goal.

This makes your role your first agreement (though implied) with a company, and there are numerous other implied agreements that go unspoken every day. To help your business results soar, we want to support you to make conscious agreements with your team. While this seems simple—it's actually not.

When making an agreement in business, you need to think about all the other agreements and commitments you've made (including the regular duties of your role) and the consequences of adding a new one onto your plate. And you have to do this often without much time, and while under some challenge or pressure.

Learning how to make solid team agreements is a pro-level leadership skill that transforms your effectiveness, and the results your team is able to achieve.

In the fast-paced, ever-changing landscape of business today, Self-Leadership strengthened by effective agreements will give you the ability to think and behave "ahead of the curve." This is what enables some companies to thrive while others falter.

On a pro-level team, everyone needs the freedom and safety to make agreements they are comfortable with and confident in.

Leading Edge Teams Self-Leadership Journal #2, **Power Agreements: What 'A+' Leaders do differently to generate extraordinary results!** This will address the topic of "Agreement-Based Teamwork." Watch for it Winter 2020.

Next Steps

1. Download all suggested materials in this journal and keep handy for your reference.
2. Retake the **Online Leadership Assessment Quiz** and see how working with this journal has helped you grow as an 'A+' Leader.

https://leadingedgeteams.com/leadership-assessment-quiz

Annie Hyman Pratt

Annie Hyman Pratt is the master at developing leaders and teams that drive rapid and sustainable results—so entrepreneurs can work on the strategic and visionary aspects of their business—and have the time, freedom, and the impact they desire. Annie more than 10x'd her family business—The Coffee Bean and Tea Leaf—taking it from seven domestic "Mom and Pop Shops" to an International Brand of 70+ stores, all in seven years time. She then led the company through a highly successful sale.

Annie spent the next two decades as a top-tier business consultant specializing in "Rapid Growth and Change." She has since worked with 50+ companies—in diverse industries—guiding them through virtually every challenge and growth stage imaginable. No other leadership or team development consultant comes close to Annie's level and scope of experience. Her track record of success stems from her unique approach to business strategy, structure, systems, finance, and the "missing link" of behavior that brings it all together.

Whatever challenges you may be facing in your business, Annie has likely already seen it—and solved it. Some of Annie's current clients include fast-growing, high-level entrepreneurs like: Jeff Walker, Lisa Sasevich, Susan Peirce Thompson, Erico Rocha, Christian Mickelsen and Reid Tracy.

Annie holds a Bachelor of Arts, Phi Beta Kappa, Magna Cum Laude, from UCLA in Economics/Business, is a licensed CPA, and holds a Master's degree in Spiritual Psychology from the University of Santa Monica.

About Leading Edge Teams

Leading Edge Teams has an unparalleled track record of helping businesses achieve massive, sustainable, TEAM-DRIVEN GROWTH...

What sets Leading Edge Teams apart is that, unlike any other company out there, our framework provides a COMPLETE, INTEGRATED SYSTEM for sustainable business growth and performance with each part working together seamlessly to fill every possible gap in your business.

MINDSET

(But not the "positive mindset" you're thinking of...) It's about shifting away from thinking you're the center of your business, to making your desired OUTCOMES the focal point. This shifts your responsibility to creating the CONDITIONS and SUPPORT your TEAM needs to achieve them.

STRUCTURE

These are the structures, systems and processes that ORGANIZE how you think about and work within the business. These provide the foundational infrastructure that allows team members to focus on ACHIEV-

ING OUTCOMES instead of getting distracted by chaos and endless re-inventing of the wheel.

BEHAVIOR—THE PEOPLE PART

All team members taking effective action towards outcomes is how you succeed—that's obvious. Yet our human personalities, emotions, preferences and habits often drive counterproductive behavior, especially within teams. We create the ongoing "behavioral habits" with your team that help your company achieve the "high performance culture" where everyone can be relied upon to take the most effective actions to achieve results, while also demonstrating leadership excellence.

BUILD TEAMS - BANISH BURNOUT
www.LeadingEdgeTeams.com

| **Annie Hyman Pratt** | **Barbara Schindler** | **Heather McGonigal** |
| CEO / Founder | COO / Executive Consultant and Coach | Program Director / Executive Coach |

'A+' Leader Development Program and Mastermind

The 'A+' Leader Development Program and Mastermind is a training program in which Annie and her team develops your key leaders to step up, take ownership of, and drive the operations of your business—helping you achieve your biggest goals.

Through this program your leaders learn to effectively lead and manage your team—taking the pressure of team development off of you so that you can focus your energy on being an innovative visionary.

LeadingEdgeTeams.com/a-plus-leader-program

Ways to Work with Leading Edge Teams

Online Classes that teach leaders and CEOs about infrastructure and foundational pieces needed to build your team and support the sustainable success of your business. In these comprehensive trainings we address key topics such as Effective Team Meetings, Functional Organizational Chart with Roles, Hiring and Keeping 'A' Players, Onboarding and Training 'A' Players and Agreements of Leadership.

Executive Coaching is about getting the desired behaviors in place. With Executive Coaching, you get the support you need in the most customized way. In this one-on-one coaching, we look at what is happening in the moment and get great leverage to implement lasting change. The best systems and processes will fail without strong focus on leadership behaviors, which is what we're known for in our work with executives, companies, and teams.

'A+' Leader Development Program and Mastermind is a leadership development program that includes a 10-course curriculum with group coaching and a business leader mastermind, as well as individual one-on-one executive coaching to support the integration of the program's teachings. Our key programs are "Visionary Master Plan," which is our high level strategic planning approach and "Functional Organization Structure with Defined Roles". Other programs include: "Performance Management" and "Executive Team Meetings."

Rapid Implementation Programs are targeted private engagements that address specialized areas to quickly move the needle for specific outcomes. Our key programs are Visionary Master Plan which is our high level strategic planning approach and Functional Organization Structure with Defined Roles. Other programs include Performance Management and Executive Team Meetings.

Customized Consulting Engagements are a custom designed way to bring Annie Hyman Pratt and her executive coaching team into your company. Engagements are crafted for the specific focus needed to up level your team and business outcomes. Our private client engagements are longer term and incorporate the infrastructure, the team/people and the behavioral pieces, and the visionary piece. This high-end business consulting is usually for larger companies with more complex or advanced situations, which Leading Edge Teams addresses very specifically with a plan for rapid implementation.

What Our Clients Say

Andrea Almarez, Vice President, The Invisible Close

This program has helped me immeasurably, growing my confidence as a leader, in my critical thinking skills, understanding everything from reading P&L statements to really being able to navigate complex team situations, giving team feedback, one-on-one and in group settings—having the real skills to navigate challenging situations that come up in everyday business.

Working with Leading Edge Teams has really given me scripts and core skills to be able to work with my CEO so that we stay in sync; that we are leading in the same direction in our teams.

We work with so many great people, but that doesn't stop challenging situations from happening and having to have difficult conversations; whether it's with a team member, or a vendor, or your peers. The things that I've learned here have really given me the confidence to navigate those in a compassionate way that also gets results.

Michael Cazayoux, CEO, Working Against Gravity

I'm a sports guy, and so I always think of things through that lens. I think when I started working with Annie I was acting as more of a one man band trying to persuade and push my team, and through working with her for the past few years I feel like we are a well-oiled machine. We now have tons of leaders working in their unique abilities; all working together to produce something 10x bigger than I could have done by myself.

One of the biggest shifts that we've gotten from working with Annie has been me not having to feel like I have to manage people anymore. Our leaders have actually turned into leaders who are managing their own teams, and I just rest assured that we're moving towards our goals, because they are every bit as capable as I am now.

Steven Gomez, CTO, Bright Line Eating

My biggest win from my learnings with Leading Edge Teams is my ability to see all the pieces in my department, as well as the company overall, look at those spots of opportunity for growth, work with the individual team members, and really present a forward thinking plan. It gets the whole department and company on the same page. It really excites the team and really inspires ownership and responsibility towards that goal.

From several of the foundational things that I've learned over the last year, I'm able to not only look at my own areas of growth, but help identify and inspire those areas for those around me. A big piece of that is operating from a level of higher self and removing any kind of defensiveness or reactiveness in decision making.